Alain Daniélou

(Shiva Sharan)

SACRED MUSIC

Its Origins, Powers, and Future

Traditional Music in Today's World

Articles selected and presented
by
Jean-Louis Gabin

INDICA

Translated from the French by Ken Hurry
except where otherwise stated

The articles included in this book are part of
The Mleccha's Exercise Books (see page 9)

Cover illustration: Gandharva. Duladeo Temple, Khajuraho.
Photo by *Raymond Burnier*

Published in 2003 by
   Indica Books
   D 40/18 Godowlia
   Varanasi - 221 001 (U.P.)
   India
   E-mail: *indicabooksindia@gmail.com*

ISBN: 81-86569-33-2

Printed in India by First Impression, New Delhi
011-22059669 - 9811224048

CONTENTS

III. THE SOURCES OF FUTURE

6

Alain Daniélou playing the Vīṇā. Rome, 1978. Photo : J. Cloarec

THE MLECCHA'S EXERCISE BOOKS

The first book to be published by Alain Daniélou, in 1936, was a selection of articles entitled *Le Tour du Monde* [1].

Since that time, over half a century ago, besides the works listed at the end of this volume, Alain Daniélou wrote hundreds of articles for journals, encyclopaedias, conferences, radio programmes, etc., which he did in various languages, Hindi, French, English, Italian.

These texts deal with a great variety of subjects concerning India, its religion, society, language, music and so on. Many can no longer be found. With the author's consent and, up to his death, under his supervision, I deemed it would be useful to publish them according to their subject matter, whence the idea of *The Mleccha's Exercise Books*.

In the languages of India, a Mleccha is a barbarian who is not born in the sacred land of India. In traditional society, a foreigner, whatever his origin, is assimilated to the caste of the Shudras, artisans and labourers, which is the most numerous caste in India, representing nearly 80% of the Hindu population.

As Alain Daniélou explains in his Memoirs, *The Way to the Labyrinth* [2], this status, which was his for many long years, is in no way a barrier to knowledge. He could study with the Pandits and Brahmans in Banaras so long as he observed the proper rules for a good Shudra student, including vegetarianism (which is not usual in

---

[1] Republished by Flammarion in 1987.

[2] *The Way to the Labyrinth. Memoirs from East and West. Autobiography*, New Directions, New York, 1987.

this caste), taking a daily ritual bath in the Ganges, never touching his master, nor entering certain parts of his house, and so on.

Alain Daniélou became a disciple of the renowned *sannyasi* Swami Karpatri. He studied traditional cosmology and metaphysics with Pt. Vijayanand Tripathi, and the vīṇā with Pt. Sivendranath Basu for several years. On Swami Karpatri's orders, he was initiated into Hinduism with the name Shiva Sharan.

Jean-Louis Gabin became involved in this project when Daniélou was still alive and has undertaken the task of collecting, editing and presenting the various texts, which are complementary to Alain Daniélou's books, providing a better understanding of his thought and his approach to contemporary problems.

This book contains the articles of *The Mlechha's Exercise Books* dealing with the subject of music. The complete *Exercise Books* will shortly be published in French.

Jacques E. Cloarec
Le Labyrinthe, September 2002

ALAIN DANIÉLOU
AND THE MUSICAL RENAISSANCE

What strikes the reader right from the start about this collection of articles and conferences by Alain Daniélou, brought together here for the first time, is their ardent and scholarly character — scholarly and concerned with clarity, as well as the breadth and variety of approaches to musical phenomena.

The very extent of these approaches directly foreshadows the variety of the music he examines. References to African music and Voodoo are given a position that is not found in reading Daniélou's major works,[1] or at least not as emphatically as in the texts for international conferences included here. A few explicit sentences on *Cante Jondo*, *Negro spirituals* and jazz thus extend the visible field of application of his thought, which one might imagine to be exclusively related to India, or to India and the western world.

There appears with great clarity an ideal of coexistence, harmony, natural influences, and reciprocal reinterpretations in the genius of each culture, against the standardising pace of what is nowadays termed globalisation.

"The ancient world was multi-cultural. The contributions of one civilisation to another took place, like trade, on an equal level, the Hindus employing Greek craftsmen, the Chinese enjoying Burmese orchestras, and the Mongols influencing Persian art."

Thus, once again, Alain Daniélou's lively and stimulating works

---

[1] See the detailed musical bibliography at the end of the volume

11

teach a lesson of tolerance, yet an active tolerance, one of curious pleasure, of understanding other systems, penetrating their logic, and of learning to appreciate their beauty.

"The fact that the knowledge of some world cultures is not expressed in the inadequate and often antiquated terminology of a western musicology still in its infancy does not mean that it may not represent a more thorough analysis of musical achievement and of the audio-mental phenomenon of sound perception."

Furthermore, the ardent, pugnacious character of certain passages illustrates the importance of Daniélou's struggle, from the beginning of the sixties, to defend, rehabilitate, and — in many cases — to save original music threatened with extinction by "harmonic aggression" [2] and attempts at "folklorising". One is struck by the clarity of the positions stated by Daniélou, sometimes even at the heart of the citadels of standardisation, as shown by the text of his conference in Moscow in 1971. It should be remembered that at that time the most demonstrative section of western intelligentsia actively protected Soviet ideology, and that it took great courage and independence to dare criticise the methods and aims of those who were creating the "radiant future". "Folklorisation is one of the most perverse methods of depersonalising national cultures under the pretext of taking an interest in them."

What does not always appear in reading Daniélou's other works on music is that, in struggling for the survival and nurturing the rebirth of a way of human civilisation that is on the point of disappearing, the author was fighting to make his readers and listeners aware of the inherent dangers that threatened their own universe:

"Tradition is inevitably the basis on which innovations can develop. Change, if it results in the loss of tradition, is more often than not a loss rather than a gain." [3]

He emphasised the fact that attacks against modal music and, more widely, against non-written orally-transmitted music, would bring no benefits to the western musical system.

---

[2] Title of one of the articles in this book.

[3] Moscow Congress, 1971 (see Chapter 5).

Indeed the latter, in its erudite forms "fixed by writing", was dying of sclerosis and intellectualism, while as far as attempts at syncretism are concerned, made despite the differences in the systems, and "decorative" borrowings, Daniélou compared them to the conduct of a child, imitating the sounds of a language it does not understand.

What comes from certain texts is thus a real cry of alarm for the West:

"We are the semi-conscious partners of an enterprise to destroy musical languages, which could be — even for ourselves — a future source of enrichment and renewal. Does this mean that, subconsciously and collectively, we do not believe in the future?"

We might find it surprising that studies on a subject that is often considered frivolous could so frequently and easily reach the domains of ethics and philosophy, but that would mean forgetting the main quality of these collected texts. Always starting from clear premises, with precisely limited notions illustrated by examples, they always lead to the essential, to what Plato, Pythagoras, or the Indian theorists never lose sight of: the fact that music is closely linked to metaphysics. At all stages it reflects and expresses the very processes of revelation, the origin and ultimate reality of which, for traditional thinkers as for the most advanced researchers in astrophysics or quantum mechanics, is vibration.

The vibration of singing, the sinusoidal character of NDA, the waves of the sea, the rhythm of Shiva's drum, the beating of the heart of the universe are the circular voices, the hands that clap at night on the banks of rivers, trance-singing, the hypnotic rhythms of the gods in ecstasy breathing on the dull bars of the mind.

We are reunited in the world of music that Daniélou saved. Nowadays, we have thousands of recordings, artists travel around the world and huge audiences rush to hear them. And this great treasure — with which we can no longer do without, no more than our forefathers after the first travels towards the East could not do without pepper and spices — can be admired just as the illuminated maps of discoveries were in the past, in the texts collected in this exercise book.

Jean-Louis Gabin

~1~

THE ORIGINS OF SACRED MUSIC

The Sacred

It is not easy to determine the limits of what we call "sacred", since the notion of sacred is applied to material forms considered as supports in the manifestation of supernatural powers, the perception of the transcendent or divine. The higher forms of religious experience are beyond the sacred and are often in opposition to it. Mystics show great indifference to observances, rites, "sacraments". In its highest forms, theirs is a direct experience of an essence whose manifestations alone constitute what is sacred. This is why the notion of sacred is so intimately tied to cosmological theories and to the language of symbols through which it is expressed. The mystic way is thus totally different from the way of ritual and sacraments to which the notion of sacred belongs.

Essentially, the sacred originates with the recognition of a directing consciousness beyond apparent forms. The elements that reveal or "symbolise" this consciousness represent the inner logic underlying the appearances of created forms. They are common to the different aspects of the manifest world and express certain data about the creative modality. Such elements may thus serve as intermediaries between mankind and divine thought, of which the created world is an expression.

This is why the sacred lives through symbols, to which magical values are attributed, since they create the possibility of a link with the divine. In actual fact, such symbols must comply with certain basic data concerning the structure of the universe. If they are merely

15

conventional, we enter the domain of the falsely sacred. In fact, the permanence and universality of certain symbols, as well as their utilisation in efficacious rites, means that they may be considered as precise interpretations of the processes of manifestation of the Creator's mind, as indications of the structures that influence the supernatural states of being that show through certain aspects of the created.

We may ask what are the bases of such symbols and how efficacious they are. Do they — and this is the basic question about the value of the sacred — form a sort of bridge between mankind and supernatural forms of being, or is their nature merely conventional and their action one of psychological suggestion?

As stated by all the philosophers of antiquity, whether Hindu, Greek, Egyptian or Chinese, it is in non-articulated sound — and the forms of music in particular — that we shall find the most obvious key to symbols and to the means of communication with the supernatural, since sound is the most abstract of our perceptions and musical sound is the most abstract form of sound expression.

It is in music that we can directly perceive numerical ratios, which we feel as expressive values, ideas, or movements. In musical structures, we may thus find the key to the relationships that unite the qualitative and quantitative abstractions expressed by numerical ratios on one side, and by the structures of matter, life, thought and sensation on the other. Indeed, relationships, harmonies, appear to be the only basic reality of all matter and all appearance. Whether atoms or stellar systems, the formation of crystals or the development of living beings, all can be traced back to the relation of powers that can be expressed by proportional numerical facts. The mechanisms of our perceptions, or of our emotional reactions used to perceive and react to the external world, necessarily follow parallel laws. It is on such bases that Hindu philosophers have concluded that matter and thought are identical, the world being a divine dream perceived as a reality, and matter being merely appearance.

Sound structures, in which physical vibration reunites emotional feeling and thought, are thus both the most powerful tool for the supernatural world beyond perception to manifest itself and at the

16

same time the means through which mankind can become aware of the supernatural world and be integrated with it.

The "word", the primordial sound (*nāda*), is the prime cause of the world, the origin of all manifestation. Sound forms, and music in particular, are thus essential at all rites, initiations, direct contacts with "spirits" and their prophetic manifestations. They play a fundamental role in the relation between mankind and the sacred.

Dance, through which rhythm becomes one with man's vital mechanisms, is a highly important tool in direct contacts between mankind and supernatural powers. Many magic rites of possession and incantation are based on the influence of musical rhythms on the subject's vital rhythms.

We shall therefore find that sound forms — and particularly musical forms — are used as the basis for all man's relations with the sacred, whether such forms are fundamental, with a direct psycho-physiological action on the human being (and at the same time a power of evocation, an action on the supernatural forces with which they allow contact to be made), or whether the presence of music is merely symbolic, like flowers, lights or incense, contributing to the creation of a "sacred atmosphere" that helps mankind to forget material worries and feel the presence of the divine. Can music be an instrument of knowledge, or simply an atmosphere that prepares for it? It is between these two conceptions that the approaches to sacred music are split.

To discover the origins of religious music, we must go back to the earliest periods of pre-history. We forget all too easily the extreme antiquity of mankind, its cultures and rites, the vast racial migrations, simply because we have "historical" documents only for a relatively very short period.

Running through the eastern and western worlds, we can discover successive layers of common culture, and also cultural migrations. This allows us to classify the forms of religious music into a set of main groupings. It is often difficult however to decide what role much more ancient forms might have played in the formation of the traditions of religious music with which we are familiar. The Aryans certainly did not "invent" Vedic psalmody, neither did the Jews Hebrew psalmody, nor the Byzantine Greeks Christian liturgical chant. They merely took over, continued and adapted much more ancient forms, whose traces can be found at every level of culture throughout the whole world.

It is in this context that we can follow in both East and West the common origins and reciprocal musical influences throughout the length of history, since the ancillary phenomena of religious expression, such as rites, chants, and holy places, are of an extraordinarily permanent nature and are wholly independent of the beliefs of any particular period.

The forms of religious music can be classified in very precise categories:

1) Noises or complex sounds, without melodic form or definite rhythm, serving to create an atmosphere of sacred terror.
2) Predominantly rhythmic forms used as a basis for sacred or ecstatic dances.
3) Psalmody, or chanted recitations of sacred texts.
4) Chanted hymns, derived in each culture from both scholarly and popular forms.
5) Forms of scholarly modal music employed as a means of inner concentration and spiritual realisation.
6) Forms of royal and martial music expressive of splendour, employed in civil and religious ceremonies.
7) Forms of scholarly music in the profane style, created to lend grandeur to religious ceremonies.

These forms or vestiges of them can be found in all religions, sometimes in folk survivals, and at other times in highly developed and refined art forms.

Complex Sounds

Complex sounds employed to create a sacred atmosphere come from the most ancient prehistoric civilisations. They are encountered among the pre-Aryan and pre-Dravidian peoples of India and of the

18

Malay peninsula, who belong to the same ethnic group as the Australoids, as well as in Europe and among the Pygmies of Central Africa. It forms part of a prehistoric animistic basis common to the West, the Middle East, India and south-east Asia.

The use of gongs and drums in Laos, in India, or in southern China, the use of "*sarvavādyam*" (in which all the instruments are made to sound together) in the temples of southern India, the use of horns in Tibet, the use of a battery of drums, hand-bells or bells at the culminating moments of the rite, are all vestiges of this very ancient tradition that requires a sound atmosphere to create a tension that favours contact with the supernatural and chases away maleficent spirits. The band of drums in the circus while acrobats are performing a dangerous exercise is a similar vestige. In cultures that we term "animistic" because the presence of the supernatural is constantly perceived in the forms of the visible world, the "temple" is merely the place set aside for dance and music, which insulate the participants from the dangers of the outer world and create a safety zone.

In the ancient forms of animist religion, such as those found among the most ancient peoples of India, the only forms of music with a sacred character are those relating to dances and magic rites. Their melodic forms are extremely simplified, whereas their hypnotic rhythms, on the other hand, are extremely complex and highly developed. It is from these archaic forms that the rhythms of religious dances probably come, creating the states of collective mystic inebriation found in all other religions, the Dionysian *mania*, the Muslim *zekhr*, Tantric Hinduism, etc.

Dionysian Shivaism

The ancient Shaivite religion of pre-Aryan origin, to which are related the Dionysian rites of the Graeco-Roman world, gives much space to music and dance as a means of communicating with the supernatural, and as the principal means of expressing divine love. Shaivite sects thus practise music and dance as an inevitable accompaniment to religious life, rites, processions, and funerals.

Neither canticles nor psalmody are involved, but proper music forms that can be more or less complex, having developed according to the cultural level of the related social group.

A very important aspect of Indian religious music coming from the Shaivite and Dionysian tradition is the "song of praise" (*bhajana*), a word that means "participation". The "participants" (*bhakta*) are the god's devotees, corresponding to the Dionysian *bacchants*. When the chant is collective, it is called the "chant of glory" (*kīrtana*), and is a synonym of the Greek "dithyramb". The *bhajana* forms one of the fundamental aspects of Indian religious life, as well as of Indian vocal music, which almost always has the characteristics of a *bhajana*, elaborated to a greater or lesser extent.

The *bhajana* is a sung mystical poem. It invokes an aspect of the deity, or some traits or events of his legend. The *bhajana* has been adopted by all India's religions, including Islam. All the great mystic poets have sung and composed *bhajanas*. The most famous are Jayadeva, Kabir, Tulsidas, Mirabai, Tansen, Raidas, and, in the south, Purandaradas, Tyagaraja, and so on. Indeed, for many Hindus, the *bhajana* is the essence of religious life. It is a form of externalised meditation. The rites are social events at which only exterior participation is required.

In the *bhajana* man truly concentrates on the divine, expresses his love for God and creation, wholy in communion with divine reality. India's great saints are represented as God's poets, who renounce all earthly ties, all human possessions and beg their food along the way, chanting the praises of Śiva, Kṛṣṇa, Rāma or the Absolute Being. But the *bhajana* is not for ascetics alone: wealthy merchants as well as Brahmins happily withdraw into the sanctuary of their home to sing or to listen to *bhajanas*. The greatest musicians of India (who are highly paid) are first and foremost singers of *bhajanas*, or of more elaborate musical forms based on the *bhajana* and preserving its mystic character.

Vishnuite sects have adopted the *bhajana* as an essential means of religious expression. The famous poem of Jayadeva (13th century), the *Gītā Govinda*, is merely a long succession of *bhajanas* and contributed to the radical transformation of the Vishnuite religion into a religion of love (*bhakti*).

Often, in the *kīrtanas* encountered especially in Bengal, communal song and dance play a major role in causing states of religious emotion, from which the participants emerge transformed, purified, pacified.

We find the same forces, deriving from the mystic Shaivite-Dionysian conception, in the *zekhr* of the Muslim world and in the mystic poetry chanted by the Iranians, the *Mathnavī* in particular.

Forms of Modal Music

With the use of forms of modal music as a means of inner concentration and spiritual realisation, we enter a properly so-called musical domain.

As we have already said, owing to its structure of intervals established in relation to a fixed tonic, modal music has a deep psycho-physiological effect, while mental concentration on the structures of a mode is considered as one of the most efficacious forms of meditation. In countries with modal art music and improvisation, music as a whole is deemed to be an instrument of spiritual realisation and as such has a religious character. This concept of the modes' psychological and ethical influence was common to the whole ancient world, to India, as well as Persia and Greece. It was through the intermediary of Byzantine music, grafted on to an ancient Roman base, that we have inherited the modal conception of religious chant, ecclesiastical modes and plain-chant. Although the truly modal character of Gregorian chant in particular is nowadays greatly diluted, the notion of the "mode" is kept more or less symbolically as an essential characteristic of true religious chant. There is a recent trend to rediscover the true modal character of plain-chant modes, based on eastern forms, which would give back to Gregorian chant the psycho-physiological action of the modes, and would fully justify the rules for their use, issued in the first centuries of the Christian era and kept up to the Middle Ages.

Modal structures constructed in relation to a fixed note, the tonic, allow us to appreciate the extreme precision of the intervals represented by the different notes of the mode. Furthermore, since each interval, each note of the scale (a harmonic minor third (6/5), for example) is always associated with the same sound, at the same frequency, during a performance, the feeling or image associated with the interval becomes increasingly intense, more and more evident. The same sound, repeated several times, each time awaking the same sensitive fibres, having the same meaning, causes increasingly strong psychological repercussions on an increasingly sensitised audio-mental mechanism.

This is why improvisation in the mode creates such a very intense inner atmosphere. Moreover, if the numerical elements that constitute the proportional factors corresponding to each note are chosen carefully, the mode tends to produce a state of trance, becoming a means of contact with the supernatural principles expressed in the particular proportions that define the intervals. These proportions are the same as those used for magical diagrams (*yantras*), utilised as a basis for shaping images or building temples. It is here that cosmological conception observes the link between physical vibration and mental perception, or thought. Similar ratios are used for dividing tempo in rhythms. In this case, their constituent numerical ratios with symbolic values are felt more directly. Well-defined particular rhythmic formulas are the basis for all kinds of ecstatic dance, leading to states of trance and a perception of the supernatural.

Sacred Dance

Nowadays, initiatic or magic dances are practically non-existent in the western world, although they still exist in the Ethiopian church, and vestiges can still be discerned in certain forms of folk dance.

In Asia and Africa, on the other hand, it is possible to study the technique of sacred dances, which are very widespread. Here too various levels must be distinguished in the character of the dances and the musical forms that accompany them.

a) The most basic are dances that produce ecstatic and prophetic states. They all feature particular rhythms, usually uneven, and corresponding movements that have an inebriating effect on the organism. Such dances are found throughout Africa, and among the archaic peoples of India, as well as in the Bengali *kīrtana* and the *zekhr* of the Turkish and Iranian dervishes.

b) Dances with a cosmological meaning have values that are similar to those of the magical diagrams (*yantras*) on which the layout of ancient temples was based, in India, China and in the West. Similar diagrams were still used in the building of Gothic cathedrals. Dances with a cosmological meaning are part of the ceremonial ritual at the Temple of Heaven in China, and in similar ceremonies in Korea, Annam, and Japan. In a slightly different form, the dance of the stars of the Parsees and dervishes represents the same concept. The circumambulations, the gestures of the priest during the sacrifice of the mass are probably also a vestige of these dances in the Christian world.

c) Theatrical dancing envisaged as a form of teaching the people is a fundamental concept of the Hindu theatre. It is only by amusing the people that they can be made to take an interest in the stories of the gods and benefit by the example of the heroes' moral virtues. In such cases, dance and musical technique is profane, i.e. artistic techniques, but are utilised to serve the ethical and religious content of the performance. Hindu temples used to keep considerable troupes of dancers for such spectacles. This is the origin of the legend about the "sacred dances" of India, which are in actual fact not sacred dances at all, but theatrical forms of dancing at the service of religious teaching, as were the mystery plays of the Middle Ages.

Psalmodies

The most ancient psalmodies are chanted recitations of mythological and historical texts constituting the traditional literature of peoples without writing, or who forbid its use for transmitting texts of a sacred nature. Such psalmodic forms have been maintained down to our own times, but for lack of ancient documents, it is impossible to know whether they have undergone any modification. The similarity of form observed in the most distant parts of the world seems to indicate the existence of a prehistoric civilisation whose conception of psalmody was fixed at a very early date, from which all existing psalmodies must largely derive.

The first form of psalmody about which we have precise and continuous documentation is Vedic psalmody in its four forms (each Veda has a different psalmody). This psalmody, which in certain cases is very different from the Shaivite psalmody, was established in two ways some time before the mid-second millennium BCE. The first way is an oral system of recitation, using mnemotechnical methods that make change impossible: a direct and inverse recitation, according to nine systems alternating and returning the syllables, thus creating an absolute automatism. After the adoption of writing by the Aryans, the Vedic texts were transcribed with notations using neums, accents and figures that are still in use today. The transmission of the written text is not however deemed valid from the ritual point of view. Only oral transmission passes on the magical content of the texts from one generation to another.

The similarities observed between Vedic psalmody and its other forms in the Mediterranean world, including Jewish and Christian psalmodies, do not necessarily imply an influence but common sources. In any case, such similarities confirm their antiquity.

It is not at all the same in the Far East. Buddhist psalmody, which derives from Vedic psalmody, has been adopted as such in all the countries where Buddhism has played an important role: Burma, Cambodia, Indonesia, China, Japan, etc. It is thus of much more recent origin than Indo-western psalmody.

Forms of Royal and Martial Music

Forms of royal and martial music employed as a symbol of divine power are met with everywhere. Here, social and religious rituals unite, implying the sacred nature of royalty and the royal nature of divinity. The musical forms, the gongs and drums are the same in both cases, since here social rites are not differentiated from religious ones. For the warrior chief, it is a matter of scaring the enemy, or of establishing his power against the hostile spirit world. The use of military bands and drums in processions in Spain and in certain other cases in the churches of other countries in Europe points to a similar concept.

In is particularly in the Mediterranean world, with possible extensions in Iran, that we encounter the deification of royalty, widely spread by the Roman Empire. This led to a conception of religious music and art, no longer envisaged as a magical means, but as an expression of grandeur and power. In the West, this came to a head in the production of orchestral and choral compositions — the "masses" by great composers — whose conception is the opposite of the Gregorian tradition, which in turn is close to the eastern conception. As often as not, there is no question of direct or immediate influence, but of the duration of certain concepts that, in each civilisation and each era, express their peculiar musical idiom.

Forms of Scholarly Music in the Profane Style

The use of forms of scholarly music of a profane style to lend grandeur to religious ceremonies derives from an identification of the notions of royalty and divinity, and covers nearly all western church music since the 16th century. It also exists to a certain extent in some eastern countries where concerts are performed in temples. This is an intrusion of the profane in the domain of the sacred, and implies an almost total loss of the magical and symbolic aspect of the truly sacred. In an animist culture, such a practice would appear dangerous and even sacrilegious.

It is only by extending terminology that profane art can be considered to have a sacred or even religious character. For Hindus, an image cannot be sacred or consecrated, meaning that it cannot become an instrument of real contact between mankind and the supernatural, unless it is constructed according to extremely precise symbolic diagrams and proportions. The aesthetically anthropo-morphic virgins and saints of our churches could thus not be truly sacred images from a Hindu point of view. The same principle applies to the rules defining the structure of musical forms.

It seems that all religious music originally comes from a search for sound forms that have a definite psycho-physiological effect and can be utilised to cause states of trance, contacts with the supernatural. These fundamental forms develop first into symbolic forms and then dissolve into aesthetics, constituting a kind of embellishment, with some vague kind of religious inspiration. Its basis is totally different, even in sacred art forming an integral part of the rites.

~2~

SYMBOLISM IN THE MUSICAL THEORIES
OF THE ORIENT

The word "symbol", from the Greek *symbolon*, "*I join*", indicates a bond between two parts of the same thing. Originally a sign of recognition, it has taken on the meaning of a sign evoking an essential, basic relationship between two states of existence as, for example, a universal principle and its tangible manifestation.

A symbol is thus a sign — a form, an image, a formula in sound, a colour, a gesture, a number — which can evoke a general or universal principle because it possesses a particular affinity with the principle itself, of which it is a more or less pictorial figuration, a representation that is more or less abstract.

Black may be a symbol for darkness, or ignorance; white the symbol of light, or knowledge; a dove, the symbol of peace. All writing was originally pictographic, later becoming symbolic when the pictogram was reduced to its essential elements, as can be seen in the evolution of Chinese ideograms. Writing became phonetic when the sound aspect became predominant, and the original figuration served to represent the same sound in other words with different meanings. The letters of our alphabet are themselves nothing more than the representation of possible articulations (guttural, palatal, labial, etc.) of the human vocal organ. At the same time, their combination as a word or phrase enables us to attribute a symbolic value to them. In Hindu syllabic writing, certain characters are considered as *mantras*, basic syllables representing certain basic principles (such as the syllable AUM). The symbolic characters are associated with *yantras*, or magic diagrams, which are believed to be the geometrical expression of certain characteristic cosmic principles, which we call gods.

The *yantra* may have various forms with the same meaning. One of the symbolic elements used for the *yantra* is the figure known as "Solomon's seal". It represents the interpenetration of an upward pointing triangle, symbolising the fire principle, masculine, active, by a downward pointing triangle, representing the water principle, feminine, passive.

It is the equivalent of the *liṅga*, the erect phallus, the source of life, inserted in the *yoni*, or receptacle, the feminine organ. Their interpenetration symbolises the union of opposites, source of all existence. The symbol of the cross has the same meaning: the upright bar evokes the fire principle, ascending, masculine, crossing a horizontal bar, which represents the water principle, static, feminine. A secondary symbolism is often attached to such *yantra*s. For Christians, the cross recalls the divine sacrifice, whereas universally it represents the creative principle, the source of life and joy.

Symbolism is found at different levels, according to whether it refers to substance, to the profound and secret nature of things, to their appearance or external form, or — simply — to certain underlying affinities. An animal (bull, lion), or indeed a tree (sacred fig tree) may be conceived as a form of manifestation that is particularly associated with an aspect of the divine, which may be termed an external symbol. This is also the case of the *liṅga*, or procreative organ, which is taken as the image or symbol of the creative principle. This is not true however of the *yantra* or *mantra*, whose symbolism is more abstract, more universal, and may appear as a sort of key to understanding the fundamental structures of creation, of the atom, of visible matter, of life, sensation and thought.

In the field of sound, symbolism is divided into the articulated symbols of language, the *mantras*, and musical symbols, the *svaras*. There is a parallel between articulated syllabic sounds and musical sounds: each category contains 52. Sound is considered to be the most abstract, the most fundamental of perceptible qualities, associated with the notion of ether, the principle of space, the substrata of matter.

The pre-eminence of sound comes from the fact that it exists as a vibration, energy that is manifested in time and space. If we consider sound as a sinusoid, we see it as a movement in space whose frequency, perceived as a certain sound register, depends on the hearer's alpha rhythm, i.e. on the length of time it is perceived. In fact, if we play a record at a different speed from the one used to record it, we change the duration of time, and consequently the perceived sound register. If we do the same with bird songs, we can perceive veritable conversations where previously we heard only a rapid trill. This is because the alpha rhythm of birds, their perception of time, is more rapid than ours.

Hindu cosmology considers that the principle of the universe is an energy manifested in vibratory form or periodic cycles, giving rise to atoms, solar worlds, and all forms of life and thought.

Music, which is formed by arranging the related frequencies of sound and the rhythmic division of time, is by its very nature related to all forms of symbolism. The Hindus, as well as the Greeks, the Egyptians and other great currents of ancient cosmological thought, regarded it as a kind of key to all knowledge, a means of communication between different levels of being, and consequently an essential element in any ritual, magic, psychological action, contact with spirits, demons and gods, as also with the lower worlds, the animal, vegetable and even mineral kingdoms. It is the most perfect instrument of symbolism.

In studying the meaning and role of music, we again find the three levels of symbolism, according to whether we envisage the sound matter, the sound structure or architecture, or merely its more or less conventional affinities.

Musical Substance

The invention of string instruments facilitated the practical and precise study of the relationships of the frequencies that form musical substance, since the length of the strings is in inverse relation to the frequencies themselves. The relations between tones could thus be easily analysed in numerical terms and a connection established between the tones and the geometric symbols of the *yantra*, as well as between numerical relations, sound perceptions and their associated psychological elements. Thus, emotional factors can be reduced to numerical formulas, opening astonishing horizons on to the nature of feeling and thought in accordance with cosmological conceptions. The result is a complete theory about the expressive value of numerical relationships, and their link with the various "states of mind", i.e. the 9 *rasas* (gaiety, tenderness, fear, disgust, eroticism, astonishment, heroism, anger, calm).

Music thus becomes a sort of key to the nature of the world, since it gives us numerical expressions referring to the structure of creation — energy-space-time — and to its developments of form (harmony, beauty) and perception (feeling, thought, life).

Musical studies have indeed played an important role in defining certain symbols.

The number "2", which defines the octave (the half-string, or double frequency) forms the neutral and inexpressive frame within which the scale develops. The octave is not perceived as a "different" tone, but as the same tone in a different register. This is similar to the notion of the square as symbol of the earth, of the base, of the frame of human existence.

Number "3", on the other hand, implies possibilities of difference or development. A world in which everything is relative requires the existence of two opposite poles and the relationship between them. This is expressed in the Hindu trinity and is encountered in one form or another in all ancient cosmologies. In music, the number "3" is represented by what we call a fifth, meaning the third of a string, or the 3/1 or 3/2 frequency ratio. Number "3", or the fifth, appears as the principle of differentiation, of indefinite multiplicity that allows a world to develop. While a succession of octaves always produces octaves identical to each other, the succession of fifths produces sounds that are always different, forming cycles that overlap indefinitely, in an increasingly subtle fashion, without ever producing an identical sound.

30

The cycle of fifths gave rise to a whole symbolic system, which sees its greatest development in the Chinese theory of the *Lyu*. This theory establishes the entire musical system on the succession of fifths up to the 60th, creating a complete hierarchy of values, according to their position from a given base.

In the basic pentatonic scale of Chinese music, the tonic note, which we shall call C, corresponds to the notion of centre, the Earth element, the Emperor, to naked animal species. The first fifth — G, 3/2 — corresponds to the South, the Fire element, summer, public utilities, feathered species symbolised by the firebird. The second fifth — D, $3^2/2^3$ (or 9/8) — represents the West, the Metal element, autumn, ministers of state, animals with hair symbolised by the white tiger. The third fifth — A+, $3^3/2^4$ (or 27/16) — represents the North, the Water element, winter, produce, animals with a carapace symbolised by the black turtle. The fourth fifth — E+, $3^4/2^6$ (or 81/64) — represents the East, spring, the people, scaled species symbolised by the blue dragon.

These degrees of the scale also correspond to the five elements and the basic colours: C is yellow, D is white, E is blue, G is red and A is black.

The cycle of fifths corresponds to the cycles of time, which repeat without ever returning to the same point. It is consequently possible to make a whole system of astrological parallels, predictions and magical designs.

Any error in the exactitude of the tones used in imperial music could lead to catastrophe. According to the Yo-Ki, the book of music (written circa 100 BCE):

"If the tonic is not clear, there is disorder, the prince is arrogant; if the second is not clear, there is dishonesty, the officials are corrupt; if the third is not clear, there is anxiety, the people are unhappy; if the fifth is not clear, there are complaints, the public services are oppressive; if the sixth is not clear, there is danger, resources are exhausted [...] In a period of disorder, the rites deteriorate and music is licentious, the said tones lack dignity, joyful tones lack calm. [...] When music exercises its action, [...] the blood and vital spirits are balanced, [....] the empire is peaceful."

31

Number "5" is linked with the senses, emotion, life. It is not just by chance that we have five senses, five fingers, that we recognise five elements or states of matter. The number "5" is Śiva's number, the symbolic equivalent of the phallus, the source of life. The crescent moon, as represented in all cultures, is the moon of the fifth day, which adorns the god's brow.

In music, the intervals based on the number "5" are the most sensitive ones, the most moving, and are the ones that in Hindu music essentially define the feeling of the mode.

This is particularly true of the third, E $(5/4)$, the sixth, A $(5/3)$, the seventh, B $(15/8 = 5 \times 3/2^3)$, as also of Db+ $(16/15 = 2^4/5 \times 3)$, of Eb+ $(6/5)$, of Ab+ $(8/5)$ and of Bb+ $(9/5)$, which have a sensual character, and especially of Db- $(25/24 = 5^2 \times 3/2^6)$ and Ab- $(25/16 = 5^2/2^4)$, which has a melancholy feeling.

Observation of psychological reactions to certain types of interval led to the Indian theory of the *śrutis*, categories of intervals, and to their systematic use in forming scales, or *rāgas*, corresponding to the "states of mind" and symbolising the cosmological principles, the gods.

Correspondences are established between tones, colours, the geometric shapes of the *yantras*, the *mantras* of spoken language and the entities they represent. Here the symbol is considered to have an actual affinity with whatever is symbolised. We might almost speak of scientific symbolism.

Number "7" does not appear in harmonic matter. We do not possess the audio-mental mechanism to appreciate the precise degree or to attribute a meaning to the 7th harmonic $(7/4)$, or to D++ $(7/8)$, which Archytas and Ptolemy call the maximal tone. To us, they appear merely false, unpleasant and incomprehensible.

Form

Up to now, we have considered what may be termed the "substance" of music, with which structures can be built. Such structures may also have a symbolic value.

The scales, or *rāgas*, first of all, constructed by placing the degrees of the scale in certain *śrutis*, make it possible to establish key signatures with a symbolic value. Thus, the seven degrees of the scale are associated with the seven transcendental worlds.

The modes themselves, according to their emotive meaning, are then associated with certain aspects of the world, particular virtues and deities.

In the most ancient Indian system of classification, the pentatonic modes are considered to be the basic ones, and are attributed a virile character. Heptatonic modes, which are their softer, less precise, versions, have a feminine character. Hexatonic modes are ambiguous.

Certain modes come to represent particular deities and evoke their presence, just like a picture or any other symbol. *Bhairava*, the basic mode in Indian music (C, D flat, E, F, G, A flat, B, C — a variant of the ancient pentatonic, C, D flat, F, G, E flat, C, the enharmonic of Olympos), evokes the image of the god Śiva. *Bhairavī* (C, D flat, E flat, F, G, A flat, B flat, C) is the mode of the goddess. Any ritual chant referring to these deities will utilise these modes, which are themselves a basis for meditation, for an evocation of the god. The 12 divisions of the octave, synthesised in the 12 notes of the tempered scale, have sometimes been associated with the months of the year, the apostles, etc.

There are no fixed melodic forms in strictly modal music, but in other systems certain melodic phrases can evoke particular characters, or situations. This is true of the Wagnerian leitmotif, of certain folk songs, and bugle calls. We might even say that, in the popular view, the first bars of the 9th symphony have become a kind of evocation of Beethoven. The imitative evocations of natural phenomena by Beethoven, Chopin, Debussy, Respighi, etc., cannot be considered symbols, and are, at the most, evocations. This is not the same with the Indian modes for fire, spring, or the night, which have a magic power, but are not an external imitation of natural sounds.

Rhythmic formulas and drumbeats can similarly evoke certain situations, principles or psychological states. The implicit numerical relations are similar to harmonic ones and their utilisation, as for example in causing states of trance, makes them an effective means of communicating with the supernatural.

Some instruments, thanks to the quality of their tone and mythological or historical associations, can acquire symbolic value. Thus, the hourglass drum, originally made of two human skulls, is a symbol of Śiva. The transverse flute is the symbol of the god Kṛṣṇa. The gesture that represents Kṛṣṇa in Indian dance *mudrās* is that of the flute-player. Panpipes play a role in Greek symbolism.

The harmonic groupings creating the tone of certain instruments may also have a symbolic function, or *mantra* value. The tone of Tibetan or African horns has a sacred character, like the sound of bells among the Buddhists and, later, in the Christian world. The tone of the bagpipe has a ritual and sacred role in Celtic tradition, where great importance is attached to the exact quality of the tone.

In all its aspects, therefore, music is based on symbolic elements, corresponding to graphic symbols, the *yantras*, speech symbols, or *mantras*, to images, or *mūrtis*, and to gestures, or *mudrās*. It forms a symbolic language making communication possible between the various states of being, evoking gods or demons, giving rise to states of trance and prophetic communication, or merely evoking human or mythological characters, as well as the forces of nature. Music can even be considered as the most abstract, the most fundamental form of symbolism, the key to all other symbols.

~3~

THE MAGIC OF SOUND

In every ancient country, strange tales are told relating to the power of sound. Musical Magicians are said to have built and destroyed cities, killed people and revived the dead, cured disease and made rain to fall or fire to spring forth, all through the mere power of their song. In the Arabic language, there are celebrated books on the treatment of disease through particular rāgas. There are also many such references in Sanskrit literature on music.

All this has been treated as poetic fiction. Yet we may well ask ourselves why such a fiction should be so widespread. There must have been some sort of background from which these legends originated. Even today we find that musical sounds and rhythms are used extensively by magicians and witch doctors in Africa, as well as many so-called primitive tribes in India and other far-eastern countries. We find that an instrument with very peculiar musical properties, the bell, is used extensively both in churches and in temples. We can hear sacred drums and sacred songs. Even in the most materialist and sceptical society today, a belief still lingers that musical sounds have a curious and powerful effect on living beings. Music has been tried in hospitals, factories and even on cows and other farm animals and some results have been claimed.

Such results are however generally accidental. Nowadays, everyone speaks of scientific knowledge, yet ideas are often still strangely inaccurate. A Mozart sonata can have no important or durable effect in curing illness or increasing a cow's milk yield. Its only value is diversion, amusement. Sound vibrations can have a very powerful impact on living organisms and even on inanimate matter, but for such purposes they have to be used methodically and follow definite rules. It is possible to see people break glasses by shrieking at a given pitch. Just a few men, if they wished to, could destroy a suspension bridge by making it swing at a rhythm corresponding to its wavelength. This is why in every army in the world, soldiers have to break steps on crossing a bridge. These, however, are minor effects of vibration and are easy to verify.

Accurate Music

In speaking of the effect of sound, we must be aware of the difference between organised sounds and what is generally called music. For the student of sound, most music has no important effect because it is not accurate enough. When they correspond exactly to certain ratios and certain pitches, intervals awaken a particular resonance in all elements of matter whose structure comprises the same ratio or wavelength. Here absolute accuracy is an indispensable feature. If we stray by one hundredth of a vibration, the sound loses its sharpness and produces no reaction. When certain systems of music, like western music for example, give up the fundamental accuracy of natural intervals by adopting such compromises as equal temperament, they entirely forego any possible "magical" effects, and, indeed, also most of its emotive power. Such music is bound to become more and more abstract and meaningless, as can be easily observed from the history of modern western music.

Despite a few reformers ever ready to imitate western mistakes, the higher forms of Indian music still lay stress on accuracy and, as such, represent the most scientific system of music in existence today. The ancient theory of the *śrutis* still presents a scheme of definite intervals connected with precise effects. This scheme is rudimentary and incomplete, intended only for common musical practice, but is basically correct and, with the help of modern methods and instruments, can be developed into a science that could yield surprising results.

The ancient Greeks said that music is the key to all sciences. This is still true today. The more we probe into the secrets of nature, the more everything tends to boil down to questions of vibrations, relations, or characteristic numbers. But music can lead us a step further than physics. Physics tells us that the atom of a given substance is merely a particular arrangement of a given number of electrons. This number is the key to the very nature of that substance, and all its physical properties are connected with it. In music, on the other hand, we find the same number or relation and study its properties, but we can also experience its effect as an emotion. We can discover its thought value, create the link between number and idea and thus reach the very causal substratum of all things, which is part of the nature of thought, as several modern physicists believe.

This had also been envisaged by the ancient seers of India. *Nāda*, the primordial vibration, the rhythmic movement within the divine mind, is the cause of all that exists. The different forms of existence are but the results of different *tattvas*, the different elements within the undifferentiated basic continuum.

The Supersonics

Just above the sound vibrations — when a sound becomes too high to be audible — there begins a range of vibratory frequencies, now known as supersonics. Many experiments have been performed very recently on supersonics because of their extraordinary properties. If you focus a beam of supersonic vibrations on some thin living tissue such as the ear of a mouse, the ear will be entirely pulverised and vanish within a short time, without the animal appearing to feel anything. You can kill fish in the water by making their blood emulsify. You can dissolve kidney or gall-bladder stones without injuring tissues. You can make water boil without it being hot and cook your dinner cold.

Now there is no essential difference between sonics and supersonics, between the sounds of music and the vibrations that produce such strange effects. Harmonics are the upper resonances that accompany sound and are theoretically unlimited, having repercussions from octave to octave into the supersonic region. But, and

37

this is a very great "but", to reach these high frequencies, the sound must be produced and repeated without any variation of pitch whatever. They can be accompanied only by sounds with which they have a perfect harmonic relationship. If there is the slightest difference, the harmonics above a given pitch neutralise each other and jam the vibration in a certain region that prevents any higher repercussion. This ceiling, where all the dissonant upper particles crash together, hangs like a veil above most music. In a western orchestra, for example, it is amazingly low and can be very easily recognised by the ear. It is made by the discordant harmonics of numerous instruments that are not exactly tuned to one another.

Furthermore, any sound with vibrato, such as that produced by most western violinists and vocalists, which is a constant movement between two very close sounds, produces its own jamming of harmonics and can therefore have no profound effect. In this case too, the classical Indian vocal and instrumental technique is much superior, since it aims at pure unwavering sounds and at a precise pitch. The effect of such sounds is therefore much deeper and more lasting.

Pitch and Interval

In Indian classical music, pitch and interval are strictly connected. This means that, in performing a *rāga*, once the *Sā*, or drone, has been given, the 3rd, the 4th, the 5th, all the intervals will always be at the same pitch. (This must be emphasised because it is not the case in other systems of music). Whenever the same interval, the same note appears, it will be of exactly the same frequency. It will therefore strike our nervous system in exactly the same place and, like a little hammer striking again and again, it will gradually make that place so sensitive that even unmusical people, or those not listening, or even animals, will be affected and moved in that particular area of their sensibility. Hence the power of Indian music is extremely great, as was that of ancient Greek music. This power is unknown, because it does not exist in other systems of music.

38

A Research Program

Indian music is consequently an ideal field for research into the theory of sound. By far the largest amount of previous systematic research is to be found in the Sanskrit works on musical theory and should serve as an initial background to any serious study. Even today however classical Indian Music offers the most magnificent example of the lines along which scientific music can work. It is to be regretted that most educated musicians and music teachers have a tendency to abandon the qualities of precision and purity of traditional music in order to adopt vague musical theories imported from the West and entirely inadequate and irrelevant to Indian Music.

I was fortunate and privileged to meet Pandit Omkarnathji who understood and demonstrated so well that precision and accuracy are the very backbone of musical expression. It has long been my wish to harness his wonderful practical knowledge of the magic of music with the little I have been able to gather about the science of sounds.

However, in order to be efficient, my work on sound requires accurate measuring and sound-producing instruments. It is true that, when inspired, great musicians reach a degree of precision in the intervals they use, which — if measured — appears astounding. Any systematic study and repeat experiences however have to rely on mechanical instruments to produce the desired pitch and intervals with rigorous precision for any length of time and at the desired intensity. Only then can successful experiments on living beings and inanimate matter be conducted. These are bound to produce amazing results and lead to a complete revision of modern theories on music and will most probably confirm much of what the Indian sages postulated long ago.

~4~

MAGIC AND POP MUSIC

Whereas spoken language is born of the need to communicate between man and man, rhythmic and melodic sound forms seem to have been developed with the aim of creating emotional states leading to communication with the invisible world, the world of spirits. Spoken language belongs to men, while musical language belongs to the gods.

At the outset of all cultures, we find, as an essential aspect of musical form, the utilisation of sound, rhythmic, modal and melodic formulas to create states of trance, of mystic inebriation, in which the individual gradually loses consciousness of his personality and becomes permeable to invisible powers, which may even express themselves through his mouth.

Magic rites, dances that cause prophetic states are met with everywhere in Asia and Africa, as they were formerly in Greece and Italy. They form the very basis of cult, of communication with the invisible, of man's participation, freed from his material worries, in a different non-utilitarian world.

In its more developed, more "civilised" aspects, music has long maintained and — in many cultures — still keeps, something of its original goal, which is to create an "emotional climate". It is so in India, where each *rāga* corresponds to a particular feeling that gradually penetrates the audience, orientating it towards sadness, tenderness, or aggressiveness, according to the characteristics of the chosen mode. The same can be said for Persian music, as it was for Greek music too.

What Hindu music causes by its modal forms, Balinese music seeks through contrapuntal forms. This wholly different musical lan-

40

guage is also oriented towards creating a "sound atmosphere" that will give rise to a state of euphoria, of freedom from contingencies. Certain African cultures seek the same result through complex polyrhythmics. The degree of artistic elaboration may vary, ranging from simple to highly refined formulas, but the role of musical art remains faithful to its original meaning, whatever the musical language structure itself.

It is its power to free from rational ties that gives music its deeper meaning, thus corresponding to one of mankind's fundamental needs. There is nothing surprising therefore in what we see reappear in the west after a period of dryness and logicism that tend to reduce the arts to more or less abstract aesthetical formulas without any psycho-physiological action. Now, we are seeing the need for a rediscovery of environmental music, sound forms that are not made to be listened to analytically, but to be undergone and lived, which can be joined in by dancing, and which lends the individual that isolation from the external world, communion with something mysterious and unknown. Jazz, pop and beat all represent the return of a whole culture towards another scale of values, to participation in an invisible but real world, which the logic of appearances tends to hide from us. We must not be astonished therefore if this new environmental music prepares those for whom it is part of life's experience for what might seem a kind of mystical search, an ideal of detachment from life, to the use of drugs that give ecstasy. All these things indicate the same trend, the same need for contact with a supernatural world.

Should such a trend lead us to abolish what has been the western conception of art for several centuries in Europe? Not necessarily. It was the barbarians that burned the idols. We must consider this art as a historical phenomenon, like an exceptional terminal flowering. The era of Europe's classico-romantic musical art is now over, and to the extent to which modern experiments seek only new forms and do not look back to the very reason for music's existence, they will remain an appendix of classical art and are doomed to failure. It is only in jazz, pop and beat and perhaps in some improvised forms of so-called

41

avant-garde music that we can recognise the vital basis that can bring new life to musical art.

It is unwise to be too quick in judging the sound forms that tend to create a psychological atmosphere. Since such a judgement is all too often based on theories outside the concepts of music itself, it may appear to us simple or primitive. This is not so, however, if we consider impartially all the aspects of sound phenomena. We need only compare the graphs from a melograph for the same work played by an inspired musician and by an ordinary performer to understand that these two things have nothing in common.

We tend to believe, for example, that the *zekr* music of the Iranian dervishes is merely a rhythmic and melodic form that is repetitive and primitive. Yet this very climate has seen the flowering of astonishing and exquisite Persian mystic poetry, probably the most profound, the most refined and richest poetry that has ever been written.

It is in this sense that today's music serving as a background for the hippie world must not be underestimated. It is the infancy of the first real musical revolution since the Italian *camerata*. I am convinced that the funeral march that concludes the musical "Hair" is itself one of the most important creations of contemporary musical art.

The return to environmental music, to an opening towards magic, of which — with the exception of certain popular forms — we have lost the sense since the time of the Dionysia, is a sign of a deep-rooted revolution whose repercussions will be felt in many fields other than music.

~5~

TRADITION AND INNOVATION
IN THE VARIOUS MUSICAL CULTURES

In any particular culture, what we call tradition in music is an original system of sounds perfected through the centuries as an instrument of artistic expression, communication, and psychological action. Such musical systems correspond, in fact, to a kind of language with its own vocabulary and syntax, forming a harmonious whole, serving the definitive purpose attributed to music in a given civilisation.

As in the case of spoken languages, a certain number of basic elements form the stock from which the musical system is developed. We therefore have something we can call "language" and something we can call "music". However, the relational systems between the basic articulate sounds, or the relations of pitch and duration that give rise to musical languages, vary considerably and it is rarely possible to utilise one system's set of relations in another system without totally disrupting the whole pattern and creating a meaningless jumble.

There is no known spoken language that does not show a high degree of development, and does not permit communication of the most abstract concepts. When one language replaces another, it is not because the new one is better, but simply because it belongs to a politically more powerful group.

The same applies to musical languages, all of which are the result of a long development within a certain system, each offering possibilities not found in others. The structures of musical language imply a choice of means, which determine the limitations of each language or music system. Modal systems, for example, use a great variety of expressive intervals that are unsuitable for polyphonic idiom.

All musical systems have clearly evolved with time, sometimes with a flowering of genius followed by a period of regression. There are always innovations, which may be an enrichment or, on the contrary, a distortion. Here too, musical languages can be compared to spoken languages. Some writers, poets, and orators create new expressions with remarkable audacity, whereas others illtreat the language, which then becomes merely bad French or bad English.

So long as a musical language develops following its own grammatical rules and within its own system, it can adapt itself to changes in sensitivity, or to the aesthetic notions of different periods. Real innovations, however, are rare and slow to develop.

In modern times, as a result of contacts between very different cultures, what are often considered to be innovations are merely borrowings. Some musicians try to make us accept mixtures of elements borrowed from other cultures as improvements. This is nothing new. In every period, composers have borrowed musical forms, rhythms, scales and styles from other cultures, which are deemed popular or exotic. It is important to remember that such borrowings, once they have been taken out of the sound system to which they belong, completely lose their original significance, and the effect they produce in their new context has nothing to do with their original purpose. Only total ignorance on the part of those who borrow certain elements from other systems and integrate them in their own can lead them to believe that the result has anything to do with the original. They act like someone who tries to imitate the sounds of a language that he does not understand.

Very few elements can be transplanted from one musical language to another. Most are extremely banal and of too little interest to be considered as a source of improvement. When such a mixture is enforced, it leads one system to destroy the other and reduces everything to the lowest common denominator, so that the result can be none other than bad music with no hope of further development.

If we wish to introduce certain elements from one system to another, the first thing to do is to see whether they are compatible.

44

We know, for example, that the modal system is totally incompatible with the harmonic. Any attempt to harmonise an Iranian *dastgah* is consequently an absurdity. All modal systems, whether Indian *rāgas*, Persian *dastagas* or Arab *maqams*, are perfect and complete systems of musical expression in themselves. They are extremely rich in expressive possibilities, comprise a large musical vocabulary, a complex syntax and highly elaborate rules of development. If we superimpose contrapuntal or harmonic elements on the melodic elements of a modal system, the melodic form immediately loses its significance, and the harmonic elements utilised can be nothing but extremely banal. The result is a mediocre and lifeless hybrid, with no scope for development. To call this an innovation is totally unjustified. It is merely a childish game played by incompetent musicians. Real artists of either system would not indulge in such games.

The same problem can arise between musical systems that have existed at different times in the same country. We have jazz versions of Bach, Beethoven and Chopin. Serious musicians consider this to be vandalism, like painting a moustache on the Mona Lisa. Yet they find it justifiable to utilise a *canto jondo* in a polyphonic system, without perceiving that the essential artistic quality of the *canto jondo* disappears in the process. It is even worse when they try to harmonise a Persian *dastgah*. In this latter case however, the difference between the two systems is so vast that few are sufficiently familiar with both to perceive the monstrous character of the result.

Generally speaking, until very recently, the Europeans' marked lack of interest in other cultures and their conviction that their own musical system was ahead of others had led to a standstill and to the almost systematic destruction of a large part of mankind's cultural heritage.

No known language is really better than another, or more developed. Each language has its advantages and subtleties. The same applies to music. No one system is altogether superior to any other. Each offers possibilities that the others do not possess.

For all its sophistication, European polyphony is totally incapable of creating the hypnotic states produced by complicated African rhythms, or the states of mind created by Indian *rāgas*. Each system has its own goals, linked to a particular philosophy of life, and is irreplaceable as a means of musical expression. No amount of mixture can improve a system or be seriously called an innovation.

What should be done in the modern context of a general standardisation that can only occur at the lowest level? I believe that first we should be more modest about the value of our own achievements and try to broaden our knowledge and artistic receptivity, seriously studying the traditional concepts of music found in the various cultures, even when such cultures have already been contaminated by centuries of cultural aggression.

When we speak of innovation in music, we should bear in mind that it means adding to something that already exists and not cutting something off. Indeed, most of what are termed modern innovations in this field have, in fact, led to the sterilisation, degradation and gradual disappearance of some skilful and refined musical systems.

Although no art can live without developing, a disordered experiment is not a development. A culture lives through its academies, which maintain its tradition with a view to new experiments. Neither should we forget that tradition implies a special teaching method that cannot be changed. The role of memory in the oral tradition cannot be replaced by written notation. We should be particularly careful to avoid the idea that anything that differs from our artistic conceptions is necessarily of popular origin, a kind of folklore that we can perfect by bringing it into the sphere of our concept of what music should be. It has been said that folklorising is one of the most perverse methods of depersonalising national cultures, by pretending to take an interest in them.

To sum up, we must consider that tradition is the inevitable basis on which innovations develop. Change, if it leads to losing tradition, is itself more often than not a loss than a profit.

Innovations can only occur within the limits of a given musical language, developed over a long tradition. Borrowings from another musical system are possible only if the two systems are compatible.

~6~

MODAL MUSIC AND HARMONIC MUSIC

Foreign Music in India

As with almost every other aspect of Indian culture, unnatural imports from an altogether foreign civilisation have created a conflict in Indian music. Although most conservative musicians have done their best to protect the ancient art against the introduction of foreign elements, some of the more curious have been attracted by the possibilities offered by a different system and many attempts have been made to bridge the wide gap separating harmonic and modal music and find a compromise.

This is not the first time such a problem has arisen. The new musical elements brought by Muslim invaders many centuries ago were successfully assimilated by the ancient Hindu music of Northern India. These, however, belonged to a system very akin to Indian music and their assimilation therefore presented no great difficulty. The rift between Western and Indian music is, on the other hand, a very deep one and to many seems unbridgeable. Yet, if we are to envisage the possibility of a compromise between Indian and Western music, we shall have to examine the basic theory of the two systems to see whether there are any points in common on which an understanding might be based. So far, no such common ground has been found and the two systems, which have confronted one another in every radio program for many years, have shown no signs of accommodation. We should now therefore take a look at their theory in an attempt to see whether there is any way in which they can accommodate one another, or whether they must necessarily be mutually destructive.

47

Courageous people, ready to bear pain for the sake of progress and even to call that pain a pleasure — or perhaps they no longer feel the difference — are few and there are many others who disagree with them and loathe modern "orchestras".

The Modern Orchestra

Many people think that accommodating Indian and Western music is not a problem. They believe that Western music enhances the beauty of melody by playing several sounds together, by adding to a song something called harmony, and they think that Indian music can only gain by following the same lines. Experience however does not seem to bear this out. Indian music, which can be so deeply moving when played on a solo instrument, seems to lose its qualities in precisely the same proportion as the number of other instruments added, with the result that what is produced by the so-called Indian orchestra is all too often a jumble of irrelevant noises, equally unpleasant to Western and Eastern ears. A few people, however, have turned their mind exclusively westward, where it is believed that this noise made by the modern orchestra is harmony; and that we must bear it, however painful, if we are to remain on the arduous path of progress.

The Problem of Indian Music

We should therefore try to find out why all these efforts to improve Indian music seem to be so unsuccessful. Is Indian music so backward that it is impossible to improve it and would be better left alone? Or is Indian music so perfect that improvement is a physical impossibility? Or is it that harmony is not an improvement of music, as we are made to believe, but rather a more primitive and noisy conception of music, which should be regarded as backward when compared to the more refined Indian musical art?

All these points will have to be carefully investigated without prejudice, if we are to form an impartial idea about this delicate question.

Rāga and Harmony

Herein lies the whole problem. Can music exist without the *rāga*, can we have music without harmony and can there be music with both *rāga* and harmony? This is what we shall now try to find out.

We shall first have to see which properties of sound are utilised in both systems of music and how far these different properties can work together, or whether they are in opposition to one another. In fact, as we shall see, there is very little in common between the two systems and they mix as badly as sugar and salt.

Definition of Music

What we generally call music is the more or less pleasing effect that correlated sounds produce on our ears. As Rama Amatya in his *Svaramelakalānidhi* tells us, "The assemblage of sounds which is pleasing to hear is called music". Sounds that are not related to one another do not constitute music, hence the noise obtained by beating a teapot and a saucepan cannot usually be called musical. Some people however manage to produce a rather detestable imitation of music using little bowls of water. According to the Sanskrit authors, however, although it is an art, this art is quite distinct from music. Music thus lies not so much in the quality of the sounds themselves, as in their relation to each other.

Let us now see whether relations between sounds are of one kind only, or of several kinds, and whether many of these relations constitute music, or whether only some of them deserve the name.

The Melodic Way

The most natural way for men and all other animals to produce related sounds is by using their vocal organs to utter a succession of sounds, each of which has a definite relation with those preceding and following. This is the melodic way of music. When we try to sing the fixed tune of the latest popular song without any instrument, we

49

are usually unaware of what *Sā, Re, Ga* may be, or of the laws co-ordinating the melody, and we could not say whether it is in this or that *rāga*. If any interval happens to be inaccurate, we can easily change pitch while singing and find that in singing the song a second time, we have gone higher up or lower down. We sing definite intervals one after another, and each one, like a word, convey its own meaning. In fact, however, the meaning of these successive intervals is not co-ordinated. It does not form the musical equivalent of a sentence. It is just music in the air, without much meaning. This is what Western musicians mean when they say that melody is not music.

The Need for Coordinating Elements

For the melody to become real music, we must find a way of making the different intervals a coherent whole. To do this, we must have a linking element, by relation to which our sounds will take on a permanent meaning. Once such a co-ordinating element appears, we find that each sound has a dual significance, one of which, as before, melodic, and another, which is its relation to the new co-ordinating elements. This new co-ordinating element may be of several kinds according to the musical systems known in the world today, which are the modal, the cyclic and the harmonic way.

The Modal Way

The modal way is how musical sound is co-ordinated in Indian, Arabic, and ancient Greek music. It consists of establishing a fixed sound — the tonic or *Sā* — to which all the sounds of the melody will be related. Suppose for example that we sing, in *Bilāval*, the interval *Ga-Pa*. Melodically, it is called a minor third — since *Ga* and *Pa* form an interval of one-and-a-half tones. It is therefore the exact melodic equivalent of the *Sā Ga komal* interval. Now, in relation to the *Sā* or tonic, the *Ga-Pa* interval gives us two new intervals: a major third *Sā-Ga*, and a perfect fifth *Sā-Pa*. We thus have, instead of one interval, a triangle of intervals comprising ma-

50

jor third-minor third-and perfect fifth. Now an ear trained to Indian music will hear mainly the *Ga* and *Pa* as a major third and a
perfect fifth, even if the *Sā* is not sounded, since the melodic relation of *Ga* and *Pa* — the minor third — is only a subsidiary relation. But the ear untrained in that system, like the average western
ear, will hear only the relative interval, the minor third *Ga-Pa*, as if
it were *Sā Ga komal*. And even if the *Sā* is sounded, he will tend to
make an abstraction of it as an intruder merely confusing the interval. This is why the fact that most foreigners dislike Indian music
does not prove, as they sometimes believe, that their system is more
refined, but only that they are as good as deaf and simply cannot
hear the sound relations that are the beauty of modal music, and
give it such deep meaning.

Thus, in the modal system, each note of the melody takes its
expression, its meaning, from its relation to the one fixed sound, the
Sā or tonic.

The Harmonic System

The peculiarities of the cyclic system used in Chinese music are
not part of our subject today. Thus we come to the system which, in
our own time, has come into direct conflict with Indian music, which
is the harmonic system.

We need some means of measuring the value of the different
notes of the melody. A simple system just sounds one or several
enharmonics at the same time, which will produce this element and
create for each note a relative third, fifth, etc.

This system has some advantages, but also great inconveniences.
If we keep the tonic *Sā* as a permanent feature, we shall always have
the same chord and the music will be monotonous. To make harmonic music feasible, we therefore have to change the tonic constantly. But, by changing the chord or tonic, we change the meaning
of any note. We can even make music without any melody at all
since the very same note can be a third, a fifth, *Re komal*, a *Pa*, a *Ni*,
or whatever we like to make it. In fact, the tendency of harmonic

51

music is to reduce melody to what, from modal standards, appears to be almost nil, because if the same chord continues for some time while the melody varies, it sounds dull, while if both chord and melody change together, it seems uncoordinated. Harmonic music therefore tends to have a relatively static melody and slowly moving chords.

We thus see one of the main points at which harmony and mode are in contradiction. In modes, or *rāgas*, the tonic is fixed and the melody moves. In harmonic music, the melody tends to be fixed and the tonic changes all the time. Thus, in the harmonic system, a different harmonisation of the same song completely changes its musical meaning.

Polyphony and Harmony

One of the main drawbacks of harmonic music is harmony. This seems rather odd, but is in fact true. Only very few sounds can be played together and create a pleasing musical impression and not a confused noise. Therefore polyphony, the playing of several sounds together, is mostly limited in harmonic music by harmony itself, that is, by the need for these sounds to mix together harmoniously. Harmony is therefore based on a very few intervals, which are the fifth and its inversion, the fourth, the major and minor thirds and their inversion the major and minor sixth. Beyond this, use of the tone or half tone creates dissonances that have to be used with great circumspection and must be properly framed by consonance. This brings the raw material of harmonic music to something like two dozen chords. The variety of harmonic music will therefore essentially depend on what is called modulation, i.e. changing the pitch, the *Sā*, continuously, so that each note is successively a fifth, a fourth, a third, etc. Thus, subtle shades of expression can be attained.

But since the change of tonic, or *Sā*, immediately destroys the *rāga*, harmonic music is not consistent with any sort of *rāga*. Indeed, people trained in the harmonic system can never understand what a *rāga* is.

Harmony and Mode

It is now easy to see how difficult it is to introduce harmony into Indian music, since the world of Indian music is the *rāga*, whereas the necessities of harmony immediately destroy the *rāga*.

Now it may be said that *rāgas* are very sweet and beautiful, but if they are an obstacle to the development of a higher music we shall have to give them up. This, I believe, is a profound misconception. The harmonic system is considered superior to the modal system only by a few ignorant westerners inflated with a superiority complex. If we value music, not according to the amount of noise it can produce (unfortunately the case in marriage ceremonies), but according to the quality and variety of the emotions it can convey, we shall find that modal music offers very great possibilities, greater in fact than any other system. This is not a question of arbitrary appreciation, but a matter of mere calculation. Leaving aside cyclic developments, which form a separate field of their own, music offers us as a means of expression rhythm, melody, mode and harmony. If we now make a simple calculation of how many possibilities can be used in both modal and harmonic music, the result will be in favour of modal music at more than one hundred to one. This is because, in harmonic music, melody is of necessity very poor, mode is nil and rhythm is reduced to highly simplified forms, since chords need time to be perceived and therefore do not lend themselves to any rhythmical intricacy.

If someone tells you that harmonic music is a more advanced system than modal music, you should not attack him — one should always respect other people's opinion — but you should understand that this almost amounts to saying that a bullock cart is a faster means of transport than an aeroplane, which in some cases it may be.

The Future of Indian Music

"But then", someone may say, "if Indian music has reached such ethereal peaks, does it mean that there is no way of improving it? No art can remain static. New developments are needed to sustain interest".

53

This is, of course, very true. Indeed, there are immense theoretical possibilities of development for Indian music, some of which have been explored in the past and some that may have remained so far unexplored. The question is only to proceed in the proper direction, with sufficient background knowledge of the theory of music.

Within the frame of the *rāga* system, there are great possibilities for orchestral development, which are not and cannot be harmonic, although they may come within the more general term of polyphony. In the old-fashioned accompaniments of singers using drums, *tānpūrā*, and *sāraṅgī* or *esrāj*, many effects, if properly analysed and systematically used, could lead to wonderful developments. The same is the case of some of the *śahnāī* orchestras in both North and South India. Some very striking sound effects are used in old dance music by the village *Kathākalī* in Kerala, as well as the Krishna Kali of Calicut, by the dancers of central Indian villages, or the Seraikalas and the various groups of dancers on the East coast of India, or on the Burmese frontier, in Assam, Manipur, etc. Through a proper study of these existing uses of polyphony, vast developments and, if desirable, hundreds of new devices can be added to present day music, without abandoning modal theory in any way.

Another very important source of information is found in Balinese and specially Javanese classical music, which even now keeps the orchestral forms of modal music imported from India a thousand years ago.

All these forms of Indian music include a vast amount of material for future development. Modern seekers after new orchestral forms should therefore not look towards western harmony, which both in theory and in practice is in complete opposition to Indian music.

Rousseau's View of Harmony

With regard to the merits of both harmonic and modal systems, it might be of interest to hear the views of the famous 18th century French philosopher, Jean-Jacques Rousseau, who has had a profound influence on the development of modern thought in the West and who was himself a music composer and author of a musical anthology. In his dictionary of music, he writes under "harmony":

"If we bear in mind that of all the people of the Earth, who all possess music and songs, Europeans are the only ones who use harmony, chords, and who find this mixture pleasant; if we bear in mind that, of all the nations who cultivated fine arts, not one knew this harmony; that no animal, no bird, no being in Nature produces any other sound than unison, any other music than melody; that Oriental languages, so sonorous, so musical, that Greek ears, so delicate, so sensitive, trained with so much art, have never guided those voluptuous and passionate peoples towards our harmony; that, without it, their music has such extraordinary effects; that, with it, ours has such feeble ones; that finally, it was to be the privilege of Northern races, whose organs, hard and rough, are more impressed by the shrillness and the noise of voices than by the softness of accents and the melody of inflexions, to make this great discovery and to put it as the principle of all the rules of Art; if, I say, we bear all this in mind, it is very difficult not to suspect that all our harmony is only a Gothic and barbarous invention, to which we would never have taken, had we been more sensitive to the real beauty of Art and of truly natural music."

~7~
CAN HARMONY BE INTRODUCED
IN INDIAN MUSIC ?

The acute problem of the harmonisation of Indian music has been much debated for a number of years. Great musicians have tried in many ways to develop Indian orchestras. The radio and recording companies have given obvious priority to orchestral forms of Indian music. The result of these efforts is a matter on which opinions differ. Both Indian and European connoisseurs of music tend to consider that modern attempts to harmonise Indian music are a meaningless barbarity. On the other hand, the common people have got used to orchestral accompaniments to songs and seem to have developed a liking to it.

The word "Harmony" has become fashionable and many people use it without knowing exactly what it means. If other countries could develop harmony, why could not India have it too? This is a simple way of putting the problem. We shall see that the answer is not so easy.

For the technician of musical theory, to speak of harmonising Indian music — i.e. the *rāga* — has about as much meaning as to speak of lying down as standing up. Harmony is a form of musical language in which groups of sounds, played together, convey a certain meaning that usually arises from their temporary relation to the lowest sound in the group. Each group, once its meaning has been grasped, gives way to another group, as if it were a new word, in which new relations are established with another base note, thus forming successive clusters, each conveying a different idea. In this sys-

56

tem, the tonic, the basic note or *Sā*, has to change for almost every chord to allow a certain amount of variety. Even if we try to use only two or three chords which can be built up within the scale of a given *rāga*, this alters the *rāga*'s expression because a chord such as "*Sā Ma Dha Sā*", for example, is really an inversion of the chord of *Ma* and destroys the modal character of the *rāga*.

Another very important difference between harmonic and modal music lies in how it is grasped by the mind. The difference is so fundamental that, unless they undergo a long and specialised re-education, even musicians trained in one system are incapable of understanding the other. They simply do not hear the essential of the music and can grasp only its superficial form.

In harmonic music, the group of notes that forms each chord is grasped as a single unit, like the sound of a word. Once the word has been understood, its component sounds have to be forgotten to make room for the next chord, which bears a relation of meaning to the previous one, but not necessarily one of sound. The new chord usually has a different tonic and often belongs to a distinct scale. In harmonic music therefore, the mind is trained to forget all previous sounds as soon as the meaning of the chord has been understood — or even if it has not been understood — to make room for a fresh approach to any new combination of sounds that may appear. This differs essentially from the mental process through which the *rāga* or mode is grasped. Here the expression of each sound depends on its relation with a permanent entity, the tonic or *Sā*, and the memory must keep an imprint of each sound as it appears until the *rāga* has established itself in the mind. In the *rāga* system, the relation of sound is thus successive; the chord forms itself in the mind. The great advantage of this method is that, since there is no physical friction between the actual sounds, all kinds of musical relations are possible which have great expressive value but would create dissonance if played together. Thus the modal or *rāga* system provides an immense number of beautiful expressive intervals found in a number of scales while harmonic music is normally reduced to a few neutral scales. In theory, western music knows only two models, though in practice it uses a few more.

From the point of view of the effect of the music, the modal system is much more powerful than the harmonic though it offers fewer possibilities for great masses of sounds. This is because, in this system, a given expressive interval always corresponds exactly to the same pitch during the performance of a *rāga*. The ear quickly associates this pitch with the corresponding expression and, since it is always struck in the same place, becomes so sensitive that the emotional effect of the interval becomes more and more powerful as the *rāga* develops. No such effect can be obtained in harmonic music because there is no such correspondence between pitch and interval, the same note can be successively a second, a third, a fifth, a minor seventh, or anything else. Indian music is really a form of magic, in which the repetition of particular sound-relations at a fixed pitch gradually acts upon the hearers and brings them to a degree of emotion quite unknown in any other system. Harmonic music is descriptive and architectural but has no such power. In actual fact, the two arts are so different that it is misleading to call both by the same name, since they are two completely different forms of expressive language. No attempt to mix them can ever bring results. Just by considering the basic technical differences, the change of tonic and the working of memory, we can already see how absurd it is to speak of harmonising Indian music. If the aim is to do away altogether with the ancient Indian system of music and replace it with some sort of western jazz, it is a different matter. In such a case, musicians should learn harmony, which is a different art and requires years of difficult studies. To believe that because someone has learnt to play in one system he is also qualified for the other is just like believing that because you have learnt Spanish you can teach Chinese.

So far, none of the Indian musicians who wish to introduce harmony to their music have really known what harmony was or meant; and the Western musicians who have tried to harmonise Indian tunes have been unable to grasp the meaning of a *rāga* and have no idea of its theoretical principles: the first official version of the Indian national anthem is a shocking example.

58

Of the main elements used in any music, Indian music is supreme in two, mode and rhythm and very rich in a third, melody. Here there is immense scope for development and Indian musicians are greatly in advance of any other musical system. Such supremacy should not be light-heartedly exchanged for a very low rank among the pseudo-harmonic systems.

Does all this mean that there can be no Indian orchestra? Far from it. There used to be orchestras, and there are forms of polyphony which are especially suited to Indian music. One of the great assets of Indian orchestration is, naturally, drumming. In the field of rhythm, no country has ever approached Indian standards. To hear a good Indian *mṛdaṅga* is an unforgettable experience for any musician. There used to be a large number of different drums, some with deep powerful voice, others clear and thin, which provided remarkable variations in colour and rhythm. It is even now very interesting to study the old type of stage-orchestra with its different drums, which still exists in some parts of South India, for example.

There are special instruments suited to accompany the voice, other to match the oboe, horn and trumpet. If orchestras are really necessary, why are these not used as they were in former times, instead of massing together a number of high-pitched solo instruments as is commonly done. It would be very useful if modern Indian conductors were to study seriously the modes of orchestration used in classical Javanese and Balinese music, instead of indulging in improvisations that are tolerated only because of the musical incompetence of too many of their sponsors and listeners. In any case, it should not be forgotten that, in the western system, expression requires simultaneous sounds and the solo is therefore always a fragment, the whole music requiring an ensemble. In Indian music, on the contrary, in which development is successive, the highest form is the solo, or rather, the duet of melody and rhythm. The whole music is included in these two aspects, the rest being mere ornament or stage effects pertaining to the lower forms of music.

The fact that Indian music cannot be harmonised does not mean that some form of accompaniment may not in some cases be written.

This is not even very difficult in the case of fixed songs, such as folk tunes, modern songs like those by Tagore, and even *bhajans*. If it is to be accurate, however, the writing of an accompaniment would require from the song-composer, as well as from the performers, a special training which is so far not common among Indian musicians. The whole of the Indian system of notation is intended as an aid to the memory, not as guide to interpretation. Its purpose is therefore entirely different from that of western notation. Yet, though an improvement in methods of notation would be welcome, it is not at all certain whether attaching too much importance to notation could be harmful to the musical conception as a whole, since it tends to paralyse improvisation.

Most early efforts at harmonising Indian music arose at the courts of the Rajas who, to gain the condescending approval of British residents, ordered their musicians to produce an orchestra at any cost. We know only too well how many years a peerless artist like Allauddin Khan — who should have been one of India's cultural Ambassadors and who could have won for Indian music the love and admiration of any country in the world — spent in this thankless task.

The conflict between *Rāga* and Harmony is not a new one. Before arising in India it was a problem in many countries of the Far and Middle East. In almost every case, the country's own learned system of music was neglected and gradually vanished, while the hybrid with which it has been replaced has failed to reach any kind of standard; so that countries which not so long ago were considered an important part of the world's culture are now non-entities in the musical world.

There is still time to save Indian Music, but the danger should not be underrated. There are still some great performing musicians, as well as ancient works on musical theory that could be recovered. Some institutions have made tremendous efforts to preserve and spread the great art of Indian music; they should receive much greater encouragement. The government of free India should be more aware of the fact that, before sponsoring new experiments, they should be first and foremost the custodians of the country's cultural tradition.

60

In any of the difficult fields of art and science, a country gains prominence only through its achievements, and not through the spreading of mediocrity. It should be India's natural role to lead the other countries of the Middle East and Indonesia in a crusade to rehabilitate their classical arts. At a time when the whole world is beginning to take a keen interest in the higher forms of Indian music, it should not be allowed to decay and vanish from India itself. Everyone should be aware that harmonising a *rāga* really means its destruction.

~8~
HARMONIC AGGRESSION

The ancient world was multi-cultural. The contributions of one civilisation to another, like trade relations, took place on a level of equality. The Hindus employed Greek artisans, the Chinese had Burmese and Nepalese orchestras, the Mongols influenced Persian art. The Mediterranean was a centre for the exchange of philosophical ideas as well as craftwork and artistic products from all over the world. Laws were found necessary to limit Rome's spending on luxury articles from India, South-East Asia and China.

Up to the Middle Ages and despite the decline of Europe after the dismemberment of the Roman Empire, cultural exchanges remained considerable. Even today, we do not know whether what is termed Andalusian music in North Africa is the result of Spanish influence on Arab music, or an Arab influence on the music of Spain. Musical treatises, whether in Greek, Latin, Sanskrit or Arabic, show practically the same conceptions of musical art and appear to have come from the same mould.

The great cultural shock that divided the world's peoples came from what is called the Renaissance, a period of great creativity, in which the rediscovery, often much falsified, of the ancient world, corroded the ecclesiastical structures and at the same time exploited the Church and religion as a pretext for unprecedented colonial expansion. On the musical level, we see the appearance of polyphonico-harmonic concepts and the counterpoint, which, on the one hand, allowed spectacular developments, while on the other it gave rise to musical imperialism and an unprecedented destruction of any other form of music. "Harmonic pollution", the conviction that whatever

was not polyphonic and not harmonised was merely a barbarous vestige of musical prehistory, was the instrument used to destroy all the
ancient music of the various European cultures. Like an oil slick, this
concept stretched ever further, destroying one musical culture after
the other. By the 19th century, it seemed that no form of musical art
could resist the infiltrations of the harmonic monster. Yet, at the very
moment when this edifice seemed to have reached its peak, flaws
began to sap its foundations. First the precursors, like Schönberg,
Satie, Stravinski, Webern, and Ives, followed by the prophets
Stockhausen and John Cage. While the enormous musical edifice of
Brahms and Wagner was collapsing, the oriental muses gradually regained their courage and, timidly, delicate musical flowers dared to
raise their head. This does not mean that the muses are necessarily on
the side of the revolutionaries, but, once the harmonic idol was broken, musical art no longer had any other undisputed tyrant.

Gradually, ears reopened to the sounds of nature, to bird songs, to
such very different musical languages through which men of different
races had expressed their joys and sorrows, dreams and visions, with
thirds that were not "in tune", scales that were not "tempered", combinations of sounds that flouted "the most elementary laws of harmony".

Gradually, this barbaric music, which Berlioz compared to the
howling of dogs or vomiting of cats, regained its right to life as the
noble representative of refined civilisations. It took time to eliminate
certain prejudices, to train an enlightened audience, since it was not
easy to stop a propaganda machine that had been harmonically brainwashing for several centuries. Gradually, too, began the great adven-
ture of finding the terrified and fearful survivors, the effort to inspire
them with the courage to re-emerge into day light, and face the triumphal shock of the great artist who meets his true public. Records
played a capital role in this process, by creating a gap between the
artist and his audience. Indeed, the creator can perform live in the
solitude of a familiar environment, while the listener can peruse this
art at leisure in the privacy of his own home. He can thus meditatively
prepare himself to confront the concert without any risk of upsetting
the artist by over-naïve reactions.

The fact that the harmonic phenomenon was accepted as the sole form of musical development and that it was identified with an uncontested notion of "progress" is psychologically very curious, connected to the whole western domination complex, which tries to find its justification in a faultless dogma. Whatever did not comply with western doctrines on a religious, social, ethical and artistic level could only be barbarous. It consequently became the moral duty of the European missionary, soldier, adventurer or composer to impose progress on peoples who till then had lived in obscurantism, or even to destroy them for their own good if they would not accept the benefits brought by the West. We should not forget that, in idiomatic Italian, the word "*cristiano*" still means today "man, person", with the evident implication that a non-Christian is not a human being.

It is odd to find that the notion of harmony belonged wholly to this complex, and to what extent it was employed to degrade, vulgarise and destroy the musical systems of Europe itself, followed by the countries that Europe attempted to dominate. The fact is that music is one of the arts in which human sensibilities are sharpest and also most vulnerable, since music possesses no logical defence system, remaining in the subtle dimension of intuition. Communities that have been hurt by attacks on their music are those that have the most difficulty in regaining their equilibrium, and this explains their resistance when asked to produce once more their artistic treasures. Nor for that matter should it be deemed that the process of destroying musical art by means of harmonic aggression is over. This is the case particularly in the Soviet Union where, under the pretext of progress, survivals of the great oriental musical traditions, often still at a very high artistic and technical level, are handed over to arrangers and harmonisers who, claiming to adapt them to modern taste, distort their nature in so-called "folk" orchestras or operas.

Without any doubt, the first breach in the edifice of imperial harmony came from Africa through the intermediary of jazz. By the tonality of its wind instruments, the lively quality of its rhythms and the nature of its improvisations, jazz brought entirely new elements to western music. In actual fact, the authorised deviations from the system were much more significant than musicians thought at the time, as can be seen by the total misunderstanding of values by composers who thought they were inspired by or imitating jazz. Indeed, when jazz began to adopt the modal structures that had nothing to do with classical tonality, very few musicians perceived that this was a complete change of both system and code of reference.

That part of America, which, as good colonialists, we continue to call "Latin", suffered more than any other region from European invasions. Its inhabitants lost even their name, and are called Indians as the result of a geographical mistake made by the conquistadors. Of the City of Mexico, whose unrivalled splendour was mentioned by Cortés, not the slightest trace remains. Only recently has there been any real interest in the fabulous *objets d'art* found in the excavations of these cities, destroyed but a very short time ago. Survivals are still hunted down mercilessly, the languages and music of the ancient peoples of the Americas having become the subject of studies that, at the most, are good for some linguist or ethnologist. They have been excluded from the cultural heritage of civilised peoples. Of course, important traces of pre-Colombian languages and music still exist, but efforts to bring them to the surface require a revaluation of the whole civilisation, despised and degraded by the invaders. Here, as in Asia and Africa, the best way to rehabilitate the art of threatened cultures is to re-establish their prime place in world culture, on the great stages of Europe itself. The search for authentic American artists is difficult since they have justifiable reasons for caution. Such research may however give unexpected results.

Elsewhere, in the Antilles and in Brazil, we find the opposite phenomenon: music of African origin, particularly ritual music, has in many cases been remarkably preserved, while at the same time in Africa itself, a continent more directly influenced by Europe, it is on the verge of disappearing.

Breaking with harmonic superstition not only affects contemporary music, but is in fact the end of a psychological epoch, reopening the door closed to other conceptions of musical language, as well as to other aspects of culture.

It is actually only little by little that an unblinkered audience can begin to rediscover the acoustic forms of other civilisations' musical arts. This cannot be done in a day and, as is often the case; wrong approaches have been used and adulterated art forms have been presented as authentic. Music is in this way no different from Indian philosophy, Zen, Buddhism, or Yoga. The will to understand is, however, much more important than the mistakes or obstacles met along the way. The hippie who gives himself up to the miserable life of the wandering monk, who seeks an instinctive rather than an intellectual understanding, is much closer to the mystic and to profound knowledge than is the logician who deems he can explain one civilisation in terms of another, without questioning his own set of values. It is at a musical level in particular that we can see the ease with which young people, quite detached from material ambitions, penetrate and understand the subtleties of Indian music, while eminent composers only see formulas, which they attempt to exploit by completely distorting their meaning.

In any language, the possibilities of communication and expression strictly depend on the richness of its vocabulary, and these possibilities are tied to the number of distinct sounds to which a precise meaning can be attributed. From spoken language, we know that minute differences of sound can lead our mental processes to grasp wholly different meanings. Theoretical simplifications of the sound scale, such as the tempered scale, are thus an impoverishment of musical language similar to what would be for the spoken language the suppression of sound differences pronounced in the same place of articulation, which the Sanskrit grammarians call *gaṇas*, i.e. *k, kh, g, gh*, or *t, th, d, dh*, or *p, ph, b, bh*, and so on. Taken separately, such sounds could be said to be almost incapable of being differentiated, but when they are employed in meaningful words, the difference in significance is immense. The same applies to accents, duration and relative pitch in tone languages. The theoretical poverty of the European sound system is thus extreme, while deviations from the system instinctively used by artists for the purpose of expression have never been scientifically analysed. It is, for example, very interesting to

66

measure electronically the intervals used by violinists and more especially by singers when they are emotionally involved in the music.
The scales they then employ no longer have anything to do with the
tempered scale.

European theoretical pronouncements on nuanced sound systems are singularly naïve. Leaving such abstract judgements aside,
however, this does not at all mean that sensitivity to expressive content is lacking. We will thus listen to the intense expression of what is
for us an exotic musical form, through a heightened perception of
the subtleties of the system of reference it employs, while in theory
we do not recognise the richness of its vocabulary. This is one of the
major reasons that explains, for example, the important focus on the
musical experience of India or Iran, whose expressive message is so
rich, while we are unable to recognise or classify the extreme complexity and subtlety of the means employed. We habitually consider
the richness of an idiom as the superimposing of simplified elements,
and not as the subdivision of complex elements. Modal music, such
as the music of India, is structured like a spoken language, meaning
that highly diversified elements are presented successively and are
regrouped in complex structures by memory. This implies a very different way of listening to music than the one used to perceive polyphony, but this new way of understanding is not difficult to acquire, since the mental processes are similar to the way we listen to
speech. We therefore already have the mechanisms in place and can,
with a little practice, entirely assimilate this music. This is not the
case, for example, with Chinese music, for which a much longer initiation is required, even though some of its theoretical structures are
closer to those of western music.

In our own times, musical life is characterised by the end of a
harmonic brainwashing to which we have been subjected for five centuries. Its demise will reopen for us a whole range of diversified sounds.
It is very interesting to note that our regained freedom is not only
musical, but is related to the collapse of whole value systems of artistic, religious, racial and social dogmas, which had succeeded in limiting the western mind to a one-way evolution and have ever since

67

been used as the pretext and excuse for the West's cultural and economic colonialism. The question now is whether this break with the racism that has been both the strength and destructive power of Europe will be the source of a vast extension of culture, or whether it will end in cultural hybridisation in which all values cancel each other out. If we know how to be truly polyglot and multi-cultural in music as in the other arts, we may see the dawning of a great renaissance and of true understanding among peoples.

Yet the diagnosis of this problem means establishing how far the vital structures of Asian, African and American civilisations have been damaged by western aggression and can subsequently be restored as a real force of artistic creation and not just as the preserved museum pieces of a vanished era. Much will depend on how quickly the great artists that survive will find their place on the international scene. We know, for example, that the pre-Colombian culture of Latin America is probably the most seriously affected, even though European influence there has lasted no longer than in India, South-East Asia or Africa.

At the same time, it must be recognised that, thanks to the work of Hornbostel at the beginning of the 20th century, Germany was the first western country ready to re-evaluate the musical cultures of Asia, and is still today the centre of the cultural revolution that has freed music from harmonic taboos. Germany remains the country with the most sincere and profound understanding of musical values. In certain towns and cities of Germany, the most sensitive oriental musicians have found, more than anywhere else, that understanding, that subtle accord between artist and audience that makes a concert an almost magical experience.

~9~

THE MUSICAL CULTURES OF THE EAST IN THE FACE OF WESTERN HEGEMONY

When we wish to compare or study relations between different cultures, we must first ensure that the elements we are comparing are really of the same nature. Ancient civilisations have developed conceptions of the visible world, mankind and the supernatural that are profoundly divergent, their basic terminology representing concepts that often have no equivalent in the languages of other cultures.

The reasons for man's position, the aims of life, the relationships of living beings with the visible and invisible worlds are envisaged in profoundly different forms.

What appears to be an achievement in one particular civilisation may well seem to be futile or blameworthy behaviour in another. The activities of "civilised" man are thus in each case oriented, directed by philosophical, cosmological and ethical notions that have no point in common.

We must consequently be very prudent when, on the basis of external and superficial observation, we compare ways of behaving and forms of expression that are not necessarily comparable. Employing terms used in one civilisation to describe the concepts of achievements of other civilisations is a source of confusion.

This is particularly so in the case of the word "music". In our mind, this word is so tied to what the art represents in our own culture that we are already led into error when we apply it to sound form organisations found in Asia and Africa. All our methods of analysis and classification are defeated when we seek to apply them to sound forms whose goals, implications, content and effects are totally foreign to us. We do not at all expect from music what an Indian or an Indonesian expects, and the reactions that their music produces on them astonishes us, when we are aware of them. We readily attribute such reactions to imaginary psychic effects, whereas they are produced by complex and skilful means whose nature escapes us at first, and which we only note in extreme cases when they are manifested by theatrical external signs.

Before attempting to compare connected forms, we must therefore be familiar with the underlying ideas and semiological content of musical languages, their *raison d'être*. It is here that knowledge of other cultures may lead us to reflect on our own concepts and, eventually, to revise them. What is music, what purpose does it serve, what do we expect from it, why do we perform it, to what need, what instinct does it correspond to? Like children, we tend to accept without question the objects and conventions of our own civilisation as natural, evident, ineluctable things. For a western child, a table, a chair or a fork are realities that are as clear and natural as a tree or a flower. For an Indian child, they do not exist, they mean nothing, seem wholly useless, uncomfortable and absurd. They interpret their use in a way that to us appears aberrant, not knowing to what superstition their usage can be attributed.

In order to try and understand the different musical arts, we must go back to their sources, attempt to understand how musical art was born, what were its initial forms and goals and how it has developed in different directions, corresponding to other conceptions of life, and has eventually developed or degenerated, i.e. in certain cases has lost some of its basic reasons for being and may have acquired others that are totally different, just as one uses milk to make plastic.

Naturally, we can know nothing of the earliest conditions that saw the development of language and its counterpart music, which are the essential means of sound communication. We can however establish a hierarchy among the civilisations we know to be the most ancient and those whose development is relatively more recent, where

70

to a large extent their languages and customs have been maintained. In India, for example, this is the case of the animistic proto-Australoid cultures with their Munda languages, the pre-Aryan cultures with agglutinative Dravidian languages, characterised by Shaivite or Dionysian cults, and the Indo-Aryan cultures connected to those of ancient Persia and Greece, with their naturalistic mythology. In neighbouring countries, civilisations with polyphonic concepts, such as those of south-east Asia, deriving from the magical orchestras of gongs from Laos, as well as the ancient tradition of contrapuntal chant for several voices from the Caucasus, from which western polyphony seems to have come.

In each case, the role and use of the sound means is quite distinct and development and refinement have thus gone in divergent directions.

For Sanskrit semanticians and grammarians like Bhartrihari, language and music are inseparable, possessing similar limitations and possibilities, according to our audio-mental classification mechanisms. Language and music must only have separated rather late, elements of the one inevitably existing in the other, in different proportions, as — for example — in tonal languages or those with quantitative syllables, which are rhythmical. The basic laws that govern language and music are similar. Certain aspects of communication are, of course, easier through one or another of these organised sound projections.

Among the most ancient peoples, it appears that rhythmic and modal forms were and still are a means of evoking and controlling invisible powers, of insulating mankind from the dangers of the surrounding world, and of creating safety zones. Music has an essentially practical role that is essential for the community's survival and no one may take the risk of treating it as an amusement by introducing more or less artistic elements of fantasy.

It is this second cultural group, which in India corresponds to the agglutinative Dravidian languages that are related to Sumerian, Georgian and probably to the pre-Aryan languages of Europe, that appear to have developed a deistic conception of the world, in opposition to the previous animistic conception. It was at this point that

71

the Shaivite religion developed, of which the Dionysian cults are a later western branch, whose hymns are still the basis of the various religious liturgies in the Mediterranean.

In the Shaivite world, music became an essential part of ritual and developed as a refined art, the principal instrument of a certain form of spiritual life. Śiva is represented as the creator of musical art, and his devotees the *bhaktas* used modal thought and its developments as a means of inner concentration and perception of the supernatural. All "scholarly" music in India and Iran still today pursues this musical ideal that shapes the inner man, harmonising and improving him, drawing him towards an inner pursuit that insulates him from material worries. It was out of opposition to this musical mystique that early Christianity and, later on, Islam showed their hostility to music, or at least to certain of its forms, to the extent of adhering to ritual formalism and to moralism as opposed to the mysticism in which human love and divine love tend to be identified.

Through its psycho-physiological action, music puts its participants into a state of sacred exaltation that facilitates superior perceptions, prophetic chants. Survivals of this conception of musical art exist everywhere.

It is on the level of goals, content and psycho-physiological effect of sound forms that we may attempt to establish parallels and may eventually speak of influences. Certainly, there are psychological and, we may say, magical elements, which are similar to the forms of sound intoxication sought by Africans, the dancers of Bahia, the *kīrtanas* of India, the dervishes of Iran, and certain modern dances in America and Europe, following up the series of the *Tarantolati* of Apulia and other similar forms. At the same time, from the point of view of musical grammar, and the organisation of sounds in what is termed music, there are few common elements in these different cultural groups, except for the *raison d'être* of the music, expressing itself in different idioms and sometimes utilising certain mechanisms.

The conception of the long chanted recitation probably developed in the world of nomads, such as the Aryans and the Semites. Reading and reciting poetry is a wholly modern concept. Poetry is everywhere linked to psalmody, chant and rhythm, and the musical element lends strength to the words, a quality and subtlety that the words alone could not express. Even in the West, we know quite well at what point, in expressing the essence of poetry, *Lieder* do something that integrates with our sensitivity, becomes a part of ourselves. Whether by Schubert, Fauré or Duparc, the music contributes an extraordinary element to a poem, in terms of understanding the meaning of the words.

Among all peoples, chanted recitation has long been the vehicle of tradition and history. It is through the bards that we have inherited Homer, the Vedas, the Purāṇas, and the Mathnavī. If we still had bards, the gods and heroes of Greece would be just as present and alive in people's minds as those of the Rāmāyaṇa or the Mahābhārata for Hindus and Indonesians.

Thus, if we wish to understand something about musical languages other than our own and obtain real enrichment from them, we must carry out some absolutely fundamental research on the nature of sound language, on the possibility of our ears to perceive and of our brain to classify sounds, as well as our psycho-physiological reactions to sound phenomena. We must also realise that in most cases, music is a language, a means of communication, and its content, its semiological aspect, directs its form. We must distrust grammarians and musicologists who try to analyse external forms without taking into account the directing thought that has shaped the forms themselves for extremely precise ends. We risk losing the essential.

Naturally, like painting, music can be limited to decorative forms, aesthetically satisfying ensembles, since aesthetics are also a form of thought and expression. It is difficult however to approach forms whose expressive goals are wholly different, whose content is of another order, with a much more direct and more powerful effect on the listener.

We may well listen to the drums talking in the African night, just as we listen to the song of the nightingale, but our imitation will lack any meaning, having nothing to do with the transmission of a message. If we truly undergo some influence on the musical level, it will challenge all our ways of thinking and living. Nothing is more enriching. But we must not confuse this kind of discovery of a world of expression that is new to us with the wholly external borrowings of forms that have been emptied of all content.

All civilisations in the ancient world, like those of the East, have established and developed their musical art on the basis of extremely precise observations of the effect of sound phenomena and ratios on human sensitivity, thought and behaviour. Music has always aimed at causing certain reactions, developing certain tendencies and aptitudes, and communicating ideas and feelings.

Western music appears to be unique in that it has no defined goal, basing its theory on physical or acoustic details of sounds that are moreover very approximate, rather than on their potential as a vehicle for some communicable content.

This fundamental difference explains the reciprocal lack of understanding of (non-depersonalised) orientals and westerners in assessing musical values. It also explains why, in view of historical circumstances that have ensured the predominance of western countries over those of the East and of the fact that international relations have been set up on a western basis, European music has been so incredibly destructive to the music of other continents and why this destruction has been unconscious and in good faith.

Even nowadays, the observations we seek to make, the so-called reciprocal borrowings or influences of which we speak, are of an astonishing naiveté, furnishing proof of a lack of fundamental data on the nature of the different musical systems.

When we speak of influence at the level of cultural values, we must consequently pay attention to the limitations set by our possibilities of comprehension and to the inexactitude of our terminology. Imitation, absorption, assimilation are not synonymous terms. They imply very distinct relationships among cultures. There are basic difficulties in understanding and digesting modes of thought and aesthetic concepts that are unusual for us, of which we perceive the form and not the content. At the same time, inter-cultural relations cannot be envisaged as being one-way, but as reciprocal action. Expanding

74

cultures become insipid. Isolated cultures suffocate. Acculturation is more often than not a poison rather than a stimulant. Hybrid cultures are rarely creative.

The incoherence, incompetence and egocentricity of cultural policies in western countries has caused the systematic destruction — first in Europe and then within an increasingly widening radius — of the musical environment, as it has of all other forms of environment, whether ancient cities, customs, landscapes, or even the air we breathe. The borrowings that may have taken place among the ancient musical traditions of Europe, then extended to Asia and Africa, were mostly acts of vandalism. They represent a sort of pillage, never a disinterested appreciation of art forms different from our own, which would be a true widening of our cultural horizon.

Western composers who have taken an interest in the musical traditions of Europe, Africa and the East have played — especially the greatest of them — a disastrous role with regard to the very traditions they claimed to be in some way reviving. What they have done in actual fact was to borrow some external mannerisms, ignoring all the basic values of any musical language outside western polyphony.

At the same time, in the same spirit in which some of our cathedrals have been preserved and turned into museum pieces, ethnologists have recorded a few old grandmothers, hoping that they will die so that their institutes can possess a unique document of a lost civilisation. Their research is always based on the conviction that polyphonic-harmonic music represents absolute progress as compared to all earlier theories, whose interest is thus strictly archaeological and historical.

I believe that, as a general rule, we may consider that up to now the influence of the various musical cultures of the East on western music has been, leaving aside the latter's prejudices and approach, relatively insignificant, limited in fact to a few inconsequential "pieces" in Turkish or Chinese style.

However, the very process involved in these superficial borrowings, together with the conviction — exported with extreme virulence — of the superiority of the musical system developed since a few centuries in Europe has been a powerful weapon of destruction of the richest and most valid musical languages of the East.

Eastern musicians have even been persuaded of the need to imitate such imitations to win a place in the contemporary musical world. The models they have been given are Debussy, Falla, Bartok, Kodaly, without mentioning Ketelby. What has been totally overlooked is the fundamental error of conception: these musicians found a source of inspiration in living and continually renewed traditions, and utilised a few elements taken out of context to create "musical themes" that could in no way replace the living stream of a continuous musical creation.

The East's importation of a terminology adapted only to western musical conceptions has led to attempts to transform this terminology for use, even if the results are aberrant. Terms such as orchestra, conductor, chorus, polyphony and harmony, applied to a system in which modal improvisation is essential, under the absurd pretext that they are the ineluctable terms of "civilised" music, has led to the creation of those unspeakable formations that are rife on the radios of India, Iran and the Arab countries, as well as the detestable "folk orchestras" of the southern republics of the Soviet Union, where the musicians, who are often highly trained, are used contrary to all the standards of their artistic tradition.

We must however acknowledge that, for some years now, the cultural revolution that has appeared among the young people of many western countries has opened a door — albeit very strait — onto a true perception of the nature and potential of the various musical languages. Today we can see young westerners who perceive the artistic potential and means of expression of these systems that differ totally from those of the West in their structures, means, goals, and expressive potential, just as we find Japanese who think entirely in the contemporary western musical idiom.

Whereas a specialist of the old school of Turkish music was able to write in a work published by us that "only indigenous ears can detect the tiny nuances of interval that distinguish the Turkish mode" (which in European terms would be like distinguishing Bach and

Chopin), several young western sitar players are today totally at ease in performing Hindu modes in their subtle complexity. Such cases of bilingual skill seem to be the only ones that could lead to a relative assessment of the different musical systems.

However — and this is where the problem arises — studying a foreign language does not lead you to modify your mother tongue. *Franglais* * is a bastard idiom spoken by illiterates. If it comes about that certain forms of eastern music acquire European citizenship, it will be parallel to and perhaps to the detriment of western musical tradition, a turning of the tables on the current expansion process wholly directed from West to East. In any case, we may hope that co-existence will be possible in the current world context, that different conceptions of musical art can flourish side by side, without breaking the most sublime works of the musical art of India and Indonesia into tiny fragments to give a little local colour to western compositions.

True co-existence, however, the widening of the concept of what music can be, the use of different sound tools to provoke artistic emotions or psycho-physiological reactions, could lead to a more proper and more human conception of musical art as a whole. From this point of view, it is not by borrowing, but by extending our conception, that the widely different musical art of Asia may one day lead the West to a more real, more profound and more universal appreciation of an art that is today reduced to experiments without any logic and without any future. I profoundly believe that the West needs other musical nourishment to regain the vitality of its own musical genius. Our main care today should be to ensure that the sources do not dry up.

---

* Pejorative term for French spoken by modern media in which a heavy quantity of English words are freely introduced (Editor's note).

77

~10~

MUSICAL NATIONALISM AND UNIVERSAL MUSIC FROM THE POINT OF VIEW OF EASTERN COUNTRIES

Although we are rarely willing to recognise the fact, even in the West itself we see that very often developments in contemporary music follow a natural aesthetic evolution. We allow ourselves to be borne along by a kind of fatalism, a feeling of duty and development, towards a new kind of music that is neither natural to us, nor — as often as not — pleasing, believing it to be nonetheless inevitable, just as the citizens of socialist countries accept a form of life that often deprives them of the pleasure of living, as the expression of an inevitable development towards the future conditions of human life.

Very few of us would dare to say, after the effort of listening to contemporary music, whether abstract or concrete, electric or mechanical, that they would really not be sorry to be lulled instead, while driving around in the traffic, by some idiotic Italian or French song, some kind of folklore, an insipid reflection of the music of the 19th century, which comes to them from their car radio. The public at large remains nostalgically attached to these antiquated forms, whose language, poor though it may be, is not considered as belonging to our own time.

If we observe musical development in the Eastern countries, we see that its causes have nothing to do with aesthetics, but are the effect of a psychological crisis leading to a depersonalisation and de-nationalisation that are the trademark of all contemporary art. This is because the driving power behind new music is not the broadening of limited musical concepts towards vaster and richer forms, but on the contrary involves their limitation to anti-national, anti-individualistic and anti-particularistic elements. Moreover, if we reflect on the psychological consequences of this trend, we shall see that in many — if not all — cases, it represents an out and out cultural suicide to the profit of inhuman abstractions. In the collective consciousness, this may be viewed as a premonitory sign of the general suicide of humanity as a whole.

The first phenomenon we find in musical developments in Asian countries is the fear of being "different", historically connected with the political, economic and industrial predominance of the West and its religious and cultural imperialism. Not to dress, speak, eat, drink, think and believe like Westerners means being an inferior, ridiculous and provincial person, or even a savage. This feeling of inferiority covers the whole set of values, customs, and morals, even when what one is about to sacrifice is a much more developed, refined and "modern" form than the proposed western replacement.

The first steps towards this evolution are purely theoretical and semantic. At all costs, orchestras are needed, conductors, composers, and so on, even when improvised monodic musical forms are involved. The result is absurd, aesthetically and emotionally revolting, but these magical terms from an international vocabulary must at all costs be applied to national music. To this effect, governments give strict orders to the radio networks, set up music schools and create those strange hybrid orchestral groups claiming to utilise national musical tradition, and seeking to persuade themselves that this is a natural development that caters for the unexpressed needs of the contemporary listener. This kind of music, which we hear in most Arab, Indian, Chinese and even Japanese films, possesses none of the technical characteristics of western polyphonic technique, but can be described using the international terminology of whose criteria it is unaware.

The second development stage arises with young musicians trained at western conservatoires, who then work, often with the aid of third-rate western composers, at orchestrating their national music, of whose principles they are entirely ignorant. We then see the

79

appearance of musical forms with an idiom close to that of 19th century European music, but employing the melodic forms and rhythms belonging to traditional oriental music. It is at this stage that the music gets written down, the resultant works resembling folk arrangements, or uses of folk themes quite close to the ones we know from various European countries, especially from Eastern Europe.

The third stage is the total abandonment of traditional idiom in order to produce purely western contemporary musical works. Only at this stage is the oriental musician granted a real place on the world scene, becoming the equal of his persecutors, with his symphonic works played by orchestras throughout the world. He wins prizes in international competitions and, having become totally denational-ised, he achieves an equality of rights on the international scene.

Does this new music interest oriental listeners? Probably not more than one in a million. But it does interest governments and their propaganda services, with the result that modern composers receive advantages and honours out of all proportion to those received by the greatest musicians who persevere in their own national musical idiom. Great efforts are needed to impose this new music on the public who, lacking any other choice, unwillingly end up being re-signed to it.

The result of this development is the wholesale abolition of au-tonomous cultures. At the same time, it is made easier by the fact that the international musical ideal is becoming more abstract, leav-ing the smallest area possible for sensitivity, emotion, or aesthetics in which there could be a risk of characteristics of racial or cultural personality reappearing. This also sheds light on musical evolution in the West itself, where we no longer have German, Italian, Spanish or French music, but a global art, experimental, strictly international and abstract.

Music, whose origins are tied to language, to expressing human emotions and feelings, developing highly different and highly com-plex idioms that provide increasingly subtle and profound forms of expression, is suddenly deprived of its main role and is banished from its original purpose. The new forms of acoustic architecture are a new art, which has very few connections with what was formerly called music. Concrete or electronic music, despite its vaguely scientific pretensions, wholly annihilates the audio-mental phenomena on which all musical languages were originally constructed. It pursues a different goal from its original one of seeking to develop musical idioms.

In countries where music is written, we have documents and contacts with a large part of our musical history and patrimony. The importance of modern experiments is merely relative. Yet in Asiatic musical forms very few elements can be practically transcribed. In the long term, the transfer of interest to new international idioms risks a total obliteration of autochthonous musical cultures, and with them an important part of mankind's cultural heritage. Such an event is not one that can be envisaged light-heartedly.

The extending of international horizons makes us realise that the monuments at Angkor or the temples of Egypt are just as important as Gothic cathedrals are for our own history and aesthetics. The extending of culture should bring about an enrichment, whereas for music it appears to be merely reducing it to a common denominator. We live in a period of political nationalism and cultural denationalisation. It appears that, for music at any rate, psychological and social factors are the only ones playing a part in Asian countries, replacing national or regional forms of the most highly developed musical art by an anonymous universal music.

In all likelihood, the importance that we attribute to modern musical experiments may itself be the result of psychological, social and political phenomena. We are risking a great deal however if we do not clearly analyse our impulse to collaborate in the destruction of a major part of musical realisation, whose riches we are slowly learning to appreciate. We are the semi-conscious partners of an enterprise to destroy musical languages, which, in the future, could become a prodigious source of enrichment and renewal. Does this mean that, subconsciously and collectively, we do not believe in the future?

~11~

THE MUSICAL LANGUAGES OF BLACK AFRICA

For the time being it is not possible to draw up an accurate picture of the musical languages of Africa, based on established and acknowledged facts. Too many elements are still lacking for any study to be valid. The observations collected up to now are as often as not scattered and are of local interest, based on criteria and methods that differ from musical linguistics, which envisage the phenomenon of sound communication, the possibilities offered by a musical system for transmitting a message and the nature of the message itself, free from any *a priori* aesthetic or evolutionary conception.

The aim we must pursue is, first of all, a research into the various cultural currents that have played a role in the development of African civilisations, and into the sound languages (spoken and musical) that have served as a means of communication among the different cultures. I have therefore simply sought to gather some suggestions for discussion, with the aim of establishing plans for a systematic study of African civilisations in the domain of music.

Nearly all western terminology relating to Africa, almost all its approaches — whether with good or bad intentions — almost every effort to take an interest in African countries, to "aid" them in their "development", totally ignore historical and cultural realities.

In the long run, this habit has, of course, affected many Africans themselves who, tired of seeing their cultural values ignored or misunderstood, tend firstly to keep them secret, then to forget them or seek a compromise that distorts their values.

A very eminent African, with the highest recognitions from European universities, told me recently, "I have stopped talking about it to Europeans, who cannot or will not understand the music I love, so I listen to it secretly at home, in the evenings".

The term Black Africa already makes me think. Can we really consider that the *tarikhs*, those chronicles in Arabic script so elegantly calligraphed at Timbuctu, are "blacker" that the Hedjaz manuscripts? Are the ancient psalmodies of the Ethiopian church really any blacker than those of the Benedictine monasteries in France and Italy? Are the Pygmies, who probably lived on the European continent in some prehistoric period, whose customs, rites and music so much resemble those of the most ancient peoples of India and of south-east Asia, Blacks, are they Africans? According to Basil Davidson (*Old Africa Rediscovered*, p. 23), "The rediscovery of Africa takes us a long way towards recognising the essential unity of the peoples of Africa with the peoples of other parts of the world. The 'lost isles' of African mankind are linked to the rest of humanity". The notion of colour can in no way be used as a basis for intellectual and cultural classification.

There is not a single people that has not come from "elsewhere", no form of thought, culture, religion or language that does not bear the traces of the influence of other civilisations, is not heir to a part of our common heritage.

We can only contribute to the continuation of African cultural values and recover whatever in those values represents a major contribution to world culture if we begin with an impartial study, without over-simplification, of the great migrations of peoples, the major currents of civilisation, languages, cultural, philosophical and artistic traditions that have blossomed on the African continent during the various periods of its history and have given rise to modes of thought, social institutions, and forms of religion and art which we can consider properly African and universally valid.

We speak of a "Greek miracle", of a "golden age" of India, of the Italian "renaissance", but there are African miracles too. What do we know today of the prestigious kingdoms of Monomotapa, or Prester John, of the civilisation of Benin, of Kumbisaleh in Ghana, of the Yoruba art of Ifa, of the court of Timbuctu before the town was sacked in 1333, of the Mali Empire up to the 14th century, and so on. Aerial photographs have revealed the modern-style layout of the straight streets of the forgotten city of Tonedikoiré in Niger. It is up to us to seek traces of these important epochs, since, in cultural matters, only miracles count and the traditions we consider as "popular" are often rich in the vestiges of great cultures of the past.

In mankind's very long history, there has been no continuous progress, but only uneven cycles. Evolution follows different rhythms on religious, philosophical, artistic and technical levels. Periods of great development in one of these domains do not necessarily correspond to those of other fields. What, according to the standards of our current culture, may appear to us as archaic or primitive, may tomorrow appear as avant-garde.

A reassessment of African cultural values is not an easy task, since the whole of the modern West's economic power is at the service of cultural, linguistic, religious and economic missionaries, all straining — as often as not quite unconsciously — towards a single goal: to destroy the originality of Africa so that it can be assimilated, subjugated or exploited. Terms such as "French-speaking Africa" are themselves wholly revealing. Unfortunately, it is highly difficult for Africans themselves not to collaborate in such actions, since the price they would have to pay for resistance would, as often as not, result in their own destruction.

This problem is not peculiar to Africa. Linguists complain about the opposition of public administrations as soon as they try to study dialects in any European country, since the central power always seeks to create a national or imperial unity, and to impose its language and customs on the regions it has acquired or assimilated.

Expansionist or colonialist civilisations, such as the Roman Empire, the Arabs, and nowadays Western and Eastern Europe, tend, at all levels, to destroy the character of the peoples they conquer or influence. Thus they surround themselves with satellites, which gradually lose their own character in order to become members of a vast complex, in which they will never be other than areas of secondary importance. At the same time, the conqueror himself, in destroying the originality of the peoples he annexes, also loses a source of enrichment and renewal, while in spreading his own culture he bastardises and weakens it. Countries that sacrifice their character for the immediate advantage of joining a great cultural or economic complex commit a grave mistake, from which they rarely recover. It is difficult to move the centre of a culture: each country that joins the union inevitably remains marginal and subordinate. This is why it is so important for a country to preserve its originality, which makes it a centre, on which depends the contribution it can make to general culture. A small, and even poor, country, whose culture is original, has a much wider radiation, a much greater importance than a large country whose culture has been assimilated within a cultural complex.

The basis of African culture differs profoundly from that of Europe today. Africa bears considerable responsibility for maintaining its traditions, customs, religions and arts during this difficult period in which it is adjusting to economic development (in no way related to any particular country or civilisation) and to the establishing of international contacts. It is important not to sacrifice to apparent and immediate facilities the character of a country, a culture, which are the essential basis of real independence, of a real and equal place in the concert of nations.

With regard to the musical languages of Africa, we must first establish some major basic distinctions on a historic, semiological and sociological level, concerning:

1) Cultural, linguistic and musical currents;
2) Links between spoken and musical languages;
3) The aims of sound communication.

These distinctions must be established on new and independent bases, without taking into account notions and methods that are current in other civilisations.

History is almost always written and presented by conquerors, however barbarous they may be. As Ibn Khaldun wrote, "With equal numbers, the nomad always wins". Defeated or subjected peoples lose their history. If we know very little about the history of Africa, it does not mean that Africa has not got a very rich and ancient history, nor that the memory of it has entirely vanished. The problem is the same here as elsewhere. The dominant country seeks to efface the history of its subject peoples in order to create a fiction of national unity. If we take the trouble, we can rediscover some of the events of the past, from survivals in Africa and elsewhere, but much more so in Africa, where the problem is of recent origin.

As on the other continents, imported influences and literary, religious or artistic notions have been gradually assimilated in the forms of expression that are characteristic of a race, a culture, or a civilisation. There are indubitably several types of African character, as there are Asian or European, each representing the selective development of a part of mankind's common heritage, largely owing to the fixing of cultural standards at different periods of history. Cultural conflicts are, as a rule, conflicts between different periods of the historic cycle coexisting in the same area. Greek civilisation profoundly influenced European culture, but we could have had an Etruscan, Egyptian or Celtic influence, leading to a different scale of values. A settling on periods that appear to us to be more archaic does not necessarily imply that they represent less developed institutions. Often the opposite is true.

In order to reach some kind of reconstruction of African musical history, we must first establish the influences, then identify the background on which such influences could have left their trace. Besides survivals of ancient foreign cultures preserved better in Africa than elsewhere, it is the autochthonous basis that provides the fundamental value, the contribution of the various civilisations of the African continent to general culture. We should not forget however that these African civilisations represent past or future stages of development for other continents. We must attempt to establish a map of Africa on anthropological, linguistic, sociological, religious and musical lines, to determine at what points the related data agrees or differs. Some peoples change their language but not their music, some change their religion but not their social institutions, and so on.

In most civilisations, music is not basically distinct from language. These two modes of sound communication have only been completely

86

separated in certain cultures for reasons of convenience. They continue to follow parallel rules. In all languages there are still elements of a decidedly musical character, which may be more or less marked, while, similarly, all music contains elements of articulated language.

Tonal languages, which are numerous in Africa, need determined melodic structures that are inexplicable when viewed according to other criteria. Languages with quantitative syllables imply metrical and rhythmic structures. These two aspects survive moreover in all languages, and traces can be found in the metres, intonation and accents of western languages, which could well be re-analysed on such bases.

Tonal languages, accentuated languages and languages with quantitative syllables inevitably lead to fundamentally distinct melodic and rhythmic systems, whose characteristics cannot easily be transferred from one system to another. This must be one of the basic criteria used in classifying musical systems in Africa.

There are thus musical systems that are predominantly melodic and others that are predominantly rhythmic, leading either to complex scales or to elaborate rhythms. One or other of these aspects always exists and plays a highly important role in classifying musical families.

For physiological and semantic reasons, the number of phonemes and their classifications are strictly parallel for music and language. This seems to be due to the type of nervous transmission and to the brain's classification mechanisms. This is also why all languages and all musical systems have a limited number of possibilities. The development of one aspect of language implies the neglect of another. This is the case, by way of example, in the development of harmonic ratios, corresponding to a decrease in melodic or rhythmic ratios. In musical languages that systematically utilise polyphonic elements, we consequently find impoverished scales and rhythms. A return to a more precise system of intervals, to more developed rhythmics, or to a more important role for the spoken element, will inevitably lead to an impoverishment of the harmonic system. In a musical system, it is consequently necessary first to determine the basic and secondary phonetic relationships. This is why the criteria belonging to one musical language can never be used to understand the communication possibilities of another musical language and its possibilities of expression. The basic phonems of the different musical languages of Africa seem to have been neither classified nor studied. From one language to another, they may be totally different and their concatenation wholly inexplicable in terms of another system.

Music can be a powerful tool of psychological action, a means of communication with the supernatural — and thus the expression and tool of a philosophy or religion — and at the same time a means of description, a pictorial interpretation of the outer world, a means of emotional suggestion, as well as a search for abstract or aesthetic plastic form.

Music that is oriented towards ritual or magical action, towards psycho-physiological action causing states of trance, or else to the creation of an emotional atmosphere to calm or stimulate, will be based on elements that are completely different from those of ornamental music, with more or less abstract aesthetic priorities. It is absolutely impossible to judge one of these musical conceptions according to the criteria of another. Our analysis of the musical elements of a magic rite and of their profound psycho-physiological effect on the participants is wholly different from that of art music used to express sentiments. Musical languages can only be understood after a thorough study of their base, aim and content, and not at all through their external form. This is why the so-called borrowings of one system from another are as often as not absurdities arising from superficial observation, somewhat like when we playfully try to imitate the sounds of a language that we do not know.

Our poor knowledge of the foundations of African philosophies and religions has made our approach to its musical values almost an aberration, leading to a kind of folk parody presented as a more or less primitive sort of art. What it really concerns is the communication of profound values representing a whole conception of the universe, mankind, life, and the goals of human existence. Africans possessing this knowledge usually prefer not to mention it to persons they deem incapable of understanding.

One of African culture's strange revenges has been the subtle and unconscious introduction of powerful and efficacious elements of psychomystic action that we may term African magic into the western world, through the medium of musical forms. Such elements play a highly important role in the psychological transformation of the new generations in America and Europe, but remain incomprehensible to earlier generations, since they imply a great change in the order of values. It is not merely a question of Brazilian voodoo, but also of the active elements of physiological musical action, which have been introduced through calypso, jazz, negro spirituals, etc., which is orienting the western world toward experiences of a physico-mystic order, access to which was denied to our ancestors. This is a change of the very postulates that are the foundation of logic, scales of values, leading to developments in behaviour that are among the most important characteristic phenomena of our time, a subtle revenge of a physically conquered Africa, gradually conquering the soul of its conquerors. The role that African influence has played through the subtle medium of music in the psychological development of the younger generations in several countries of the American continent could be the subject of an interesting study, if the related musical elements were studied and analysed.

Any impartial study of musical phenomena must be based on the content and role of the message transmitted. An analysis of the sound means utilised to transmit this message is only possible and only has any meaning if we know the nature of the content to be transmitted. It is thus clear that a musical language that transmits a rich content through simplified sound means is a more developed form. The idea that complex polyphony is necessarily superior to a monody from a musical point of view is totally unjustifiable. This prejudice, however, is the source of efforts made almost everywhere to add chords to monodic or melodic-rhythmic languages that are perfect on their own. The result of this kind of aberration has totally distorted any assessment of the musical languages of Africa and Asia, and is one of the main causes of their degeneration.

89

~12~

THE IMPACT OF WRITING AND RECORDING
ON MUSICAL CREATIVITY

Writing was originally a memorandum, a graphic means of fixing and storing certain thought elements for later use. In this sense, the writing of music is extremely ancient. Traces are found in the oldest known civilisations. In its most perfected forms, the writing of music becomes, not merely a memorandum, but a means of communication, allowing other individuals to reconstitute the outlines of a musical performance they have never heard.

But the writing of music, however perfect, has its limits. The role of the performer, who, on the basis of oral tradition and subjective understanding, breathes life back into the written work, is considerable. When the oral tradition is lost, reconstructions — i.e. interpretations — become extremely divergent, often distancing themselves considerably from the intention or idea of the "composer". The written arrangement thus serves as a basis for expressing other ideas, feelings other than the composer's, like an imprecise tradition.

Furthermore, the writing process gradually reacts upon the written music, tending both to eliminate from musical language any expressions that cannot be transcribed and to develop any structural elements that lend themselves to transcription.

In certain civilisations with an oral tradition, mnemotechnic means play a similar role to that of writing. Such is the case, for example, of the *bols*, the rhythmic formulas learned by heart in Indian music, or methods of chanted recitation of multiple formulas, which are employed to ensure the permanence of Vedic chant and are

90

much more effective and accurate than writing. Children therefore do not learn musical works, but formulas, similar to the elements of vocabulary and grammar through which they become familiar with the subtleties of their mother tongue. Writing tends to eliminate these methods and music is then transmitted no longer as a system, as a musical language, but from the outside.

In this latter case, musical creation is thus divided between the "composer" who thinks up a musical form and writes down what writing allows him to transcribe, and the performer, who seeks to recreate the sound form conceived by the composer.

Given the profound difference between these two approaches, it is not surprising that the musical systems of oral tradition and those of written tradition put the accent on entirely different aspects of musical language and develop along diverging and wholly incompatible lines.

This is why all efforts to transcribe music belonging to the oral tradition inevitably lead to absurd results, since their development lies in those subtle grey areas that writing cannot encompass, while the structural elements on which written music prospers are rudimentary.

Indeed any music that seeks to have a direct psychological effect, and to create an element, a certain subtlety in rhythm, embellishment and intervals, tends to repudiate the written form. In Europe, this is the case with gypsy music, flamenco and, nowadays, jazz.

Recording has provided music with a new means of transcription. In this case, it is the performance as heard by the audience that is preserved in its every detail. It is probable that, apart from schematic arrangements, writing would never have developed if recording had existed a few centuries earlier. The modern composer tends, moreover, to write directly for recording, so as not to be at the mercy of the performer, whose inventions could be a travesty of his intentions. Or else, in writing, he consciously establishes an arrangement that each musician can interpret as he pleases, thus returning to the ancient formula where the performer must improvise the development of a form of which only the outline is indicated.

For music belonging to the oral tradition, recording is unsuitable because it fixes a moment of a musical creation, which musicians will do their best to imitate like a parrot down to the last detail, leading to a fixed form that is never renewed. Skilful imitators will thus be able to provide an illusion, but their so-called improvisation in actual fact becomes a "piece" that is always the same. For the creative musician however, recording provides a useful model that allows him to become familiar with the style, methods and skills of the great masters. For the purpose of musical education, recordings have an immense value, allowing everyone to hear the great creative artists. Its inconvenience however is that it makes audiences hypercritical about technique, consequently depriving of support perfectly valid musicians who do not reach the technical level of the great virtuosi. So long as recording stimulates the practice of music and concert attendance, it is a good thing, but if it replaces musical practice among amateurs and tends to reduce live music to the professionalism of a few virtuosi, it is certainly a very bad thing.

As a part of everyday life and as a part of individual creative experience, music suffers equally both from being written down and from being recorded, but for different reasons.

~13~

MUSIC IN THE MODERN WORLD

Whereas the development of the individual, the sharpening of his intellect, the accumulation of the elements that form his culture is a gradual and continuous process, the cultural development of society as a whole takes place suddenly, in blocks, since every epoch has to establish its social and ethical laws, its religious, philosophical and aesthetic concepts, that allow a multiplicity of individuals to co-operate on a common task. Such necessary and inevitable standardisation always gives rise — though sometimes only for short periods — to conservatism, to a belief in definitively established values, which paralyses progress. This is why people whose sensitivity and thought belong to a past stage are often belittled, and those geniuses who create the future are persecuted in the name of an established order or science. Nowadays a Titian or Corot could only live as forgers, since their right to be great painters would be unrecognised. I have heard the critics of one of the best operas written in these last few years say unanimously — and with some ingenuity — "It would have been an excellent opera if it had been written thirty years ago". The opera in question, which should be included in every repertory, has only been staged a few times. As far as creators of the future are concerned, we know well how they have always been condemned in the name of the science of their own time.

It is for this reason that artistic, moral or social progress appears in successive revolutions, with all the inconveniences and excesses that revolutions bring with them. We must therefore envisage history, and that of the arts in particular, in terms of periods, more or less static epochs between two revolutions.

93

Our own epoch has brought so many new elements into the field of science, in means of communication, contacts between peoples and cultures, that it is difficult to assimilate them quickly enough to allow for any sort of logical development, or even to be able to establish a scale of values that could be updated periodically, a sort of orderly revolution.

It is thus particularly important that we should attempt, as often as possible, to make a re-estimation of values, seen from a totally impartial point of view, without taking into account what our own time considers to be established values, even if such values are the outcome of some very recent development.

From this point of view, music is an especially interesting domain, because it is relatively gratuitous. What does music mean in the modern world? What do we call music? Why is the music we prefer to listen to often considered bad music, and the music we try to understand with virtuous boredom, considered to be good? Nowadays, there is widening disagreement between popular music and scholarly music. What are the reasons for it? Is it a question of progress in an art too rapid for the common man to follow, just as he is unable to follow progress in mathematics? Or, on the contrary, is it a failure to recognise the psycho-physiological factors in an art, which, up to now, like all arts, has been primarily considered as a means of communication? In such a case, we might be led to think that contemporary music is developing on an erroneous input and is consequently a false science, a false art, an abstract game for the mind, amusing solely for specialists or scientific handymen.

The future of music will largely depend on our being capable to make an impartial estimation of our values. Of course, such an estimation will inevitably be influenced little by little by the logic of things. We should not forget however that great eras arise out of managed revolutions, avoiding long periods of transitory chaos, and that it is preferable not to waste too much time waiting for natural selection, after long years, to reach the same result as an organised selection that would take far less time.

We may try to summarise the problems and facts of music in the contemporary world, in a certain number of points.

The Progress of Technology

Music has always been a favourite field for theoreticians, whether Pythagoras, Aristoxenes, Sharngadeva, King Fang, Boethius, Zarlino or Rameau, Stockhausen, Scherchen, Boulez or Xenakis. But just as grammarians have not created poetry or the art of oratory, but have only codified the rules of language after the event, so the theoreticians do not create musical art. The very fact that they now want to make music using computers or following stochastic principles implies a failure to recognise the role of musical art as a means of communication, as a form of language serving as a vehicle for certain emotional factors. There seems to be some misunderstanding, some scientific quid pro quo. The true science of music does not lie in an analysis of certain acoustic and physical phenomena, or in mathematical formulae, but in studying the perception of these phenomena and the receptor's (i.e. the ear's) capacity of transmission to the brain. It also involves the brain's capacity to classify and analyse, since the brain does not operate solely on a certain logical input, but requires a semantic content, a message, to understand and assimilate the elements of the musical language. The human brain is first and foremost a utilitarian organ, a defence and communication tool made to interpret messages from the organs and the senses, so as to deduce emotive and defensive reactions.

In order to develop and renew itself, musical science should therefore start from psycho-physiological and semantic data, on which we possess much new information, before venturing into the field of sound experiments and mathematical applications. The experiments of musicians today as often as not merely develop and continue — without ever reconsidering the assumptions — acoustic and arithmetical conceptions dating from antiquity, which appear out of date in the light of modern psychology and physiology.

Unrest in this domain goes far back. It reached its crucial point with the adoption of equal temperament and the approximations it involves in the field of psycho-physiological data. These approximations have for better or worse made it possible to suggest — while distorting them slightly — musical forms corresponding to our audio-mental mechanism and to use them in the implementation of highly theatrical musical structures. The logic of this system was however to culminate in the neutral dodecaphony of our own epoch, which tries to make a system out of a makeshift, with results that are often totally insipid to the listener, who is not exclusively interested in theoretical data. Clearly, a creator of genius can produce marvellous works with poor tools, but an impartial study clearly shows that Schönberg, for example, could have produced great works despite his dodecaphonism and not because of it. An analysis of his works can be made just as well on other bases than his theory and show that the freeing of tonal conceptions allowed him to introduce other logical elements through the approximations of a defective system, but that the value of these elements is not at all inherent in the system itself.

The Weight of History and the Superstition of Progress

In traditional forms of music, a musician is asked to produce a beautiful, well-made moving work in a traditional idiom whose renewal and development are imperceptible.

When Gluck composed his Orpheus, he had never heard Monteverdi's. He did not even know that Monteverdi existed. His audience hardly worried about the sources he may have used. Writing, editions of past works and their increasingly widespread diffusion, as well as the superstition of progress and the cult of novelty, pose on the other hand an insoluble problem for the contemporary composer. If a hint of Debussy or Brahms, Liszt or Fauré can be detected in his work, he is lost. His work must be different. This is why it is almost necessarily bizarre and bleak, indeed highly conventional in its negative movement. The conservatism of Soviet artistic policy is often under fire. I am not at all defending it, since the State is never equipped to judge and direct the arts. But although we often speak of the sad position of the modernistic composer in the USSR, we too easily forget the sad status of the western composer, whose sensitivity is still attached to classical idiom. At the same time, it is far from certain — from the strict point of view of the work of art — that avant-garde work is necessarily superior to work that is behind the times.

However, interest in the history of music has led to the discovery and reconstruction of a great number of ancient works, which may be the most important contribution of our time to contemporary musical art. When a Milanese taxi driver, who used to buy a weekly instalment of a major history of music, sold at the price of a magazine, with a small record attached, told me, "I much prefer last week's Monteverdi record to this week's Palestrina", I realised what immense possibilities modern methods have for spreading musical culture. What was the taxi driver's musical education like? A few operatic arias from the 19th century, certainly present-day songs. And great contemporary music? "Ah, but that's not music!"

Popular Music and Avant-Garde Music

This leads us to a very important problem concerning the extraordinary division of music today. On the one side, we have dance music and songs, continuing at almost folklore level some of the aspects of classical tradition, representing the only form of contemporary music known and appreciated by the enormous majority of the population in any country. On the other hand, there is avant-garde music — making one think immediately of the rear-guard — which has completely lost contact with most of the population. This was not the case with the music of Rossini, or Verdi, or even Wagner. A dance by Brahms or a waltz by Chopin reached an almost universal audience in the western world.

This is a phenomenon that must be studied carefully and impartially. We shall discover that, even from a purely theoretical point of view, not all the advantages are on one side. Envisaged on a communication level, in some of its elements of scale and interval, its rhythmic aspects that are sometimes quite elaborate, its adjustment of melodic forms to the language input, tone quality and its sound level in relation to acoustic perceptions and improvised embellishments, contemporary song and dance music is much more developed from the point of view of audio-mental perception and semantic content, even if it is rudimentary. I should even say that it is technically much more scientific than many of today's lucubrations of serial, dodecaphonic or concrete music. The fact that the harmonics of modern songs and dances are often so mediocre and distressingly banal may perhaps be only due to the fact that the musicians one hears tend to be busy playing with their computers rather than writing for the human beings of their time. Their production tends to be a summary of experimental works, destined for small, specialised groups. In songs and jazz, we often encounter incidental harmonic ideas, development and orchestration formulas that are far from being worthless, even if their use is embryonic.

In song, as also often in folklore, we find refined forms of emotional communication, despite the rudimentary means. When a young singer like Hervé Villard sings with poignant pathos "*Fais-la rire*", nothing can stop me thinking of Fauré, going into major, to sing "*Tout en chantant sur le mode mineur*". It is the same psychologically highly effective subtle process of antithesis. Here, however, we have the artistic concept. What we must regret is that nowadays we have no Fauré to give it a less elementary form, to write songs, dances or symphonies that correspond to the psycho-physiological laws of music as a means of communication and expression for the human emotions. This is, whatever people may claim, the real goal of musical art in all cultures. In the songs of Rabindranath Tagore, we have a recent example of a great poet and musician who has completely renewed the popular song in his native Bengal.

Contacts Between Cultures

A further important element in the context of contemporary music is its unexpected contact with highly developed musical forms belonging to other cultures. Such contacts have existed to a lesser degree at various times. During the whole classical and romantic period, however, the western world was so certain of representing progress on all levels that forms of exotic music, as also what we term folklore, were considered to be some kind of raw material, from which contemporary composers could freely borrow elements of form or colour to create a certain picturesque atmosphere. Naturally, such borrowings were limited in value, because in transposing them albeit very approximately into a different idiom, they ignored the grammar of the musical languages that had inspired them. Instead of ensuring the maintenance of precious and original musical traditions, until quite recently, it was deemed sufficient to utilise some of these elements "in music", whether Napolitan songs in the case of Listzt, Flamenco for Falla or Granados, or Hungarian and Gypsy traditions for Bartok.

Even today, we find eminent musicians and musicologists who do not hesitate to say and write that they have heard "traditional Indian or Japanese musicians, who show such a great technical disposition that if schools could be organised to teach them counterpoint and harmony, they would certainly manage to produce real music".

Happily, this state of mind is tending to lose ground, and the discovery of the great musical systems of Asia will be one of the important phenomena of the years to come. It will no longer be a matter of discovering elements that can be used in our idiom, but on the contrary, possibilities of musical expression offered by musical languages that are totally different from our own, and furthermore, are often technically incompatible with our contrapuntal and polyphonic concepts.

This new opening to conceptions that are quite different as to what music is, what it can express and the means it employs, will involve a considerable widening of musical horizons, with repercussions that are difficult to foresee.

In the modern world, music is certainly in a state of crisis — psychological, technical and aesthetic — but this state, if it is not taken too seriously, can be a good thing. Modern conventionalism replacing classical conventionalism is a transitory state.

The extraordinary abundance of new data and tools at a psycho-physiological level, at the level of musical semantics, acoustics and electronics, as well as the discovery of other musical cultures, should allow us to revise our conceptions on a new basis and to achieve a music that is truly new, but also truly human.

~14~

MUSIC AND MEDITATION

Before seriously studying the relation between what we call music and what we call meditation, we need to define these terms carefully, since, as is often the case, they are rather vague and ambiguous.

The word meditation covers a variety of mental attitudes and processes and, unless these are clarified, we cannot define the kind of sound-relations in music, which can be a necessary element, help or hindrance in the meditating process.

At a first stage, meditation may be only a mental exercise, in which the constant agitation characteristic of our cerebral system is made to focus upon a particular image or idea. In this case, some kind of background music, not really listened to, may be a help in the sense that it deadens our sensitivity to other external sounds. A part of our mind is normally always on the alert for unexpected noises that could be a signal of danger, which is part of the most fundamental instincts in men and animals. A soft regular musical pattern isolates us from other sounds and thus facilitates mental concentration. This is also true for some people whose studies require an undisturbed attention.

Meditation according to Yoga techniques develops through three stages. The first consists in concentrating our thought on a particular image or concept. This is called *dhāraṇā*, a word whose meaning is very nearly that of "meditation". At a second stage, our thought becomes entirely concentrated, without fluctuation, on the object of our meditation. This is called *dhyāna* (holding or contemplation).

There is then no room for any other thought. In this state of contemplation the activities of the mind are greatly reduced. No idea

101

external to the object of contemplation can interfere and disturb the meditation. In the third stage, we become identified with the object of our meditation. Our mind becomes completely still. There is no longer any notion such as "I am meditating". It is the object of our meditation that has become our inner self. This is called *samādhi* (identification).

While a musical background may facilitate the two first stages, mainly as a sort of enveloping, protecting sheath of harmonious sound, it does not play any part in the third stage unless a sound element is part of the object of our meditation.

Music can however be an essential instrument in the meditation process, and indeed its main factor. At this point, it is music itself that becomes the subject of meditation. But not all kinds of music are suitable for this purpose. Structures of correlated sounds through which the mind can wander — we could say "improvisations" like the Indian *rāgas* — can be and are in fact a remarkable instrument for mental concentration. All Indian music, all modal music, is actually a form of meditation, since it requires inner concentration on the structure, scale and other characteristics of the *rāga*, as well as the emotional, religious and symbolic elements associated with it, which are described in poems and pictures. Such concentration eliminates any other thought. The process of music-creation through the *rāga* is nothing more than an exteriorized form of meditation.

Any transcendent aspect of the cosmic world, any deity, principle, or relation such as those we call love or virtue, or matter, or universe, can be represented in various equivalent ways that differ according to the inclination of our mind, such as, for example, a mathematical formula, or a visible form, either geometrical (a *yantra*) or anthropomorphic (the image of a divinity, whether it be Rāma, Kṛṣṇa or Christ or a teacher, but even a plant, flower, or animal). It can also be a smell or taste, but first of all a sound, either articulate (in which case it is called a *mantra*) or musical (*rāga*). A combination of articulate and musical sounds, or a sung poem, can also be a support for meditation. In India this is called a *bhajana*, a devotional song, and is very widely used as a means of mental concentration, or relaxing meditation.

Whether the structure of atomic matter, life or perception, the world contains nothing but related forms of Energy. Our senses perceive only the relations of vibrations transmitted through electric pulsation codes to our brain. Among these, the most abstract are considered to be sound-vibrations, since we can neither see, touch, smell, nor taste what we hear. It is only through sound that we can directly perceive the relations of frequencies that we express in terms of mathematical ratios or in terms of emotional content. Sound is considered the most direct manifestation of the very process by which the Universe came into existence, since it is only an infinitely complex structure of related energies and motions. Thus it is said that the "Word" — structured sound — is the principle of all things. We find the same idea in Christian theology "*In principium erat verbum ... ante omnia facta sunt*".

The higher form of meditation is therefore considered to be meditation on the principle of sound (*nāda*) which is symbolized by the sacred syllable AUM, a syllable said to include all the possibilities of speech since it is made of a guttural, a labial and a nasal sound, all other sounds being unavoidably contained within this triangle.

Meditation on AUM is however not possible at first, the subject being too abstract, too synthetic. This is why the rhythmic repetition of a *mantra*, a spoken formula with an intelligible content, is one of the recommended ways of concentration, the most abstract mantra being "*so-aham*" (I am He) in the Hindu formulation; "*Hu* (He) *Hay* (living)" in Islamic mysticism. For most people, concentration on a visible image, like the body of a divinity, is an easier process. But anything can be taken as an object of meditation, even the most material, since there is nothing in the world that is not related to its divine origin. There is a story in the *Purāṇas* about a poor cowherd who spent all his life looking after a buffalo. At the time of his death, he did not think of himself, or his belongings or children, but only of his buffalo, and what would happen to him. At the moment of dying, he simply murmured the animal's name. Suddenly the god Viṣṇu appeared before him saying "You called me, here I am". The man said, "But I only called my dear buffalo" and the god replied, "Whenever your love for anything is so strong that no other thought remains in your mind, it is me you worship". This is the ultimate aim of all meditation.

Music as the main instrument of meditative concentration and identification has been practiced by most Indian mystics. This is easier using the modal, or *rāga* system.

First of all a man must find his tonic, or basic frequency, the basic sound that is attuned to his nature and which is different for everyone. The gradual rising of the diapason, which has been happening in Europe since the 17th century, is very characteristic of our civilization, since the higher sounds are more material, further away from the slow vibrations from which the world initiates and develops. In meditation one should reach silence through the lowest sounds, which are more spiritual. The first thing a musician's apprentice practices is to determine the basic sound, the *Sā* (Tonic), which is natural to him, which comes out naturally with his breath. Once this sound is firmly established, he can gradually, one after another, find the exact subtle pitch of each note of the ascending scale of a *rāga* corresponding to a particular emotional state. Each emotional state is however the expression of a particular state of being, a particular aspect of divinity. Hence the *rāgas* will bring out the image of a particular deity. The *Bhairavī rāga* (C Db Ed F G Ab Bb C), soft and tender, is the image of the mother-goddess; the *Bhairava* (C Db E F G Ab B C), strong and sensuous, is the image of Śiva; the *Dīpak rāga*, fierce and radiant, is the image of Agni, the god of Fire, while the *Vasanta rāga* (C Db E F A B C) evokes the god of spring and love.

For the Hindu philosopher and mystic, these are not just arbitrary associations. The potentiality of anything must exist before it comes into being. The principles of space and time must exist before a spatial world may be created. The principles of love and hate must exist before these emotions can be experienced. These principles — from which all created forms derive — are what we may call divinity, the source of all that exists. The object of meditation is to bring us nearer to that inner aspect of things, nearer to fundamental reality. This is why meditation can liberate us from our everyday material

104

interests and worries, make us more balanced, more relaxed, more tolerant, and more human in the higher sense of the word.

The Indian *rāga* system, with its thousands of years of experience, has systematically correlated musical relations with sounds and other aspects of the universe, material and spiritual, all of which can be expressed in terms of ratios. This does not mean however that similar results may not be obtained through other musical systems. The inspired artist finds ways to express profound realities and truths through any musical language or form. Some of Schubert's *Lieder* convey exactly the same subtle state of emotion as some Indian *rāgas*, although their musical structures have nothing in common.

To be useful for meditation, music must however be limited to a single theme. A long composition with various movements does not facilitate deep concentration. The musical forms used to provoke states of trance in Voodoo, or in the mystical rites of India and the Middle East, are extremely limited and repetitive. They represent, in fact, a process of extreme concentration, involving not only our mental, but also our physical being, our body. Through this process, man loses control over his mental faculties and his bodily reactions, and becomes identified with a superior state of being, as if possessed by a supernatural power. It is impossible to reach such stages without the help of a highly rhythmical musical form, since our vital functions are regulated by the rhythmic beats of our heart, and the rhythmic pulsation of our brain, called the *alpha rhythm*, which determine our notion of time. Powerful musical rhythms can affect our vital balance, our perception of the space and time in which we are imprisoned. In the normal process of meditation, on the other hand, it is the harmonious and not the rhythmical aspect that is predominant.

Meditation can lead us to higher forms of knowledge, an inner knowledge that is total experience, not just a mental approximation. Thus, through the practice of mental concentration, which is part of Yoga techniques, we can *experience* the reality of a god, not merely believe in his existence. Through meditation we can establish a real contact with divinity, and manifested divinity in the world is merely rhythm and harmony. This is why, of all the Hindu philosophical systems, only Yoga is theistic, since its aim is supra-mental, leading to direct experience and not merely to mental rationalisation. It is only through the practice of Yoga, and this includes the inner experience of musical relations, that we can establish direct contact with supernatural beings and know the certainty of their reality. The highest aspect of the transcendent being that we can perceive is the "principle of sound", the *Nāda-brahman* from which the world was born. And the process through which the world derives as a complex structure of interrelated vibrations is similar to the harmonious development of musical structures. Śiva created all beings through the rhythm of his drum, the harmony of his dance and song. Conversely, we can understand the inner structure of all things and the principle behind them through meditation on the harmony of sounds.

Music in the western world has gone far astray from its fundamental purpose, and has become a merely aesthetic amusement. Yet the greatest of composers and performers have looked at music as a way of elevating the soul, of seeking wisdom. Music remains a way of escaping materialism, of forgetting our ambitions and preoccupations.

The sufis of Iran, like the *sādhus* of India, renounce the world and become wandering ascetics, whose main way of life is music. It is through music that they bring to mankind the oblivion of misery, the message of a spiritual life.

All the great poets of India, Iran and the Arab world have been mystics and musicians. All their poetry was sung.

The modal way of music, in spite of resistance due to habit and of a too limited concept of what music should be and can be, is making rapid progress among the younger generation of the western world, bringing with it a concept of music that is a search for inner peace, for a more human and more spiritual life, a music that is in itself a form, a very subtle and high form of meditation.

~15~

Music, an International Language?

There is a tendency to believe that music is a kind of international language, a common level on which different peoples can understand one another. Unfortunately, this is an illusion. There are musical languages, just as there are articulated languages, and, as a rule, it is difficult for us to understand a musical language with which we are not familiar. Studying a new musical language takes just as long and is no less difficult than for a spoken language.

If a westerner wishes to approach the music of India, he must start by forgetting whatever he knows about musical grammar or vocabulary. This means counterpoint, melody, harmony, modulation, consonance, dissonance, etc., since these terms either have no meaning or have a different one in modal music, although they refer to physical laws that clearly have equivalent applications in the two systems.

Spoken Language and Musical Language

Like language, music is a means of expressing ideas or feelings through sound. Music is in fact but one form of language, a form that utilises the related pitch or frequency of sounds rather than their articulation or repeated interruption. Rhythm, which marks these variations, is common to both poetry and music in ancient languages.

Hindu philosophers believe in the existence of a basic form of language, which they call true language, whose forms are based on the real association of sounds and ideas. Whereas the various languages departed from this original language however, music still remains close to it. This is why the forms of musical language are more directly perceptible and are also fewer than those of spoken language.

But it is always possible, both in music as in language, to replace the true forms by conventional ones, so that we obtain systems that are only intelligible to the initiated.

Chinese music is the most famous example. It is, in effect, a musical system in which the relative placing of sounds in an indefinite cycle of fifths gives them a symbolic value perceived intellectually as an idea, and not directly as an emotional feeling. Indeed, nearly all musical systems use a certain number of conventional symbolic elements that can only be understood once the conventions themselves have been assimilated. This is why, contrary to a fairly widespread belief, music is far from being a universal language accessible to all, but is on the contrary divided into different and mutually exclusive systems.

Modal Music

Hindu music belongs to the same music group as Greek music and ancient Turkish music, which became Arab music. This music group is known as modal. In its music, the vibration ratios that make up the expression, or musical "word", are formed by the relationships of mobile sounds with a fixed tone, the tonic, and other secondary tones, which are known as "dominant notes".

The belief that the modal form is a development of what is termed melody in harmonic music is a serious mistake.

Indeed, modal music only appears to be melodic from the point of view of simultaneous harmony. From the point of view of its own expression, it is quite different. To perceive modal music however, we must forget all our musical habits and acquire new ones. For example, when we hear a set of chords, we must listen to each one separately, just as we listen to successive words in a phrase. If we hold on to a chord while listening to the next one, we have nothing more than a din lacking any meaning. Our memory is thus trained to forget a chord as soon as we perceive another.

108

In modal music, exactly the opposite happens, since we have to memorise the elements formed by successive sounds, whose complex ratios constitute its musical expression. This may seem difficult, but in fact is quite easy.

This system has the great advantage of establishing extremely complex, varied and subtle sound ratios, without running into the accessory phenomenon of dissonance. It thus opens the door to possibilities of expression that are technically impossible in the harmonic system.

The Scope of Modal music

The various musical systems necessarily utilise the same sound properties because the properties themselves relate to physical laws, but they use them in different ways and consequently lead to different results. Indeed, the order of things that modal music seeks to express is essentially different from that of harmonic music. This is one of the reasons why persons used to one of these musical systems tend not to be interested in the other, since they do not find there what they expect of music. Real musicians, on the other hand, always looking for new modes of expression, are immediately attracted by the discovery of a new musical language, allowing them to express with ease a whole order of emotions or ideas for which their own language has no words.

Unfortunately, true musicians, who follow music as they would a thought, are rather rare and are often unable to break out of the closed circle formed by each civilisation and travel freely in different worlds, where arts and sciences are governed by other laws. This is why, as a rule, we only get the views of unqualified amateurs on musical systems different from our own, who can only repeat the music and not the thought.

Like all music, modal music is based on the fact that certain sound ratios have a defined impact on the nervous system and incline us, as Aristotle remarks, to sadness or gaiety, to tenderness, courage, indifference, and so on.

109

If we classify all the simple sound ratios, we can form a kind of lexicon of agreements between sounds and the ideas or feelings they arouse. Then, by combining these ratios in different ways, we can form what Hindu music calls "*rāgas*", meaning states of mind, such as sad affection or gay affection, a joyous activity or a desperate activity, dark and troubled repose or a pure and luminous night.

The essential point, however, at which modal music differs from modern western music lies in the fact that a sound ratio can only have a lasting impact on our feelings if its elements are rigorously permanent. This means that if we hear a given interval, once, for a moment, it can, if we are very attentive, delicately evoke an idea. If, on the other hand, we hear the same interval repeatedly and at the same pitch, we find that our senses gradually harmonise with it, and its resonance becomes more and more intense, seizes us more and more to the point at which we ourselves are but a reflection of the idea represented by the interval, wholly modelled by its influence.

This explains the inevitable structure of the modal system, which requires a rigorously permanent tonic pedal in relation to which a certain number of carefully chosen intervals form a series of ratios determining the desired state of mind. While the harmonic system tends to use ever more violent and brutal effects in attempting to impose an idea, an all too fugitive expression, the modal system, on the contrary, tends to form an increasingly tenuous lacework of sounds, whose effect on a sensitivity quickened by the repeated hammering of the intervals becomes gradually more and more intense. This explains why theoreticians of modal music insist to such an extent on prudence in using certain modes and intervals, precautions that appear as absurd superstitions to the harmonic musician. This is because, in actual fact, by using the modes, it is possible to produce an extraordinary effect on a listener or a crowd and, without their even paying attention, put them all into the same extremely intense state of mind. By repeatedly using the appropriate sound ratios, it is actually possible to lead a person to the deepest melancholy or even suicide, just as he can be galvanised for action, rather similar to the effect of certain modern drugs.

The educational influence attributed to music by the Greeks is thus no exaggeration, since the habitual practice of certain modes is a sure training towards certain kinds of thought and feeling.

Development of the Mode

In Hindu music, the mode or *rāga* thus corresponds both to a set of arithmetically defined sound ratios and to a state of mind. This is why the modes are called *rāgas*, a word that means precisely a state of mind.

A *rāga* is essentially defined by a fixed tonic plus a set of notes as often as not varying from five to twelve, forming the scale or gamut of the mode, and lastly by certain accents marked by the dominant of one or two main sounds that form the most important intervals and give the mode its principal character. To these data are added, for certain modes, themes and ways of approaching certain notes so as to alter their character slightly. Clearly, the character of a note always approached with the aid of an appoggiatura, or as a wave starting from a lower note, will be attenuated by the note that envelops and accompanies it.

These data impose very strict rules on the ascending or descending scale of the mode, on the arrival or departure point for every melodic figure, and on the placing of all the accents. The musician, by playing more or less skilfully with the data, by touching lightly or stressing certain feelings, builds up an invisible web that makes the form of the mode appear as a living image, with its personality and character. In Hindu theory, the mode is a real entity that exists by itself, like a Platonic idea. The musician's role is to mark in brilliant points a curve, a shape, an angle of this entity, until it stands before us fully revealed. Like that of his audience, the musician's mind must concentrate on the actual living entity itself, and not on the convolutions of sound moving from one point to another. The process is entirely similar to the way in which an artist brings a likeness into being. No one dreams of establishing the pencil's precise graphic movements on the paper, but rather the volumes and forms it seeks to represent.

111

This is why it is always a mistake to speak of modal music as melodic music, because the melodic outline is merely a secondary and ornamental aspect, on which attention should never be focused.

History and Literature

Before dealing with the technical side of Hindu music, I feel I should give a glimpse of its history. Hindu music is the only ancient musical system that has survived down to our own time, whereas Chinese music has undergone substantial transformations and alterations at different periods in its history.

For the music of India, on the other hand, we can see an extraordinary continuity both in theory and in practice from the earliest times to the present. If we leave aside the Sāma Veda texts relating to sacred music, the date of which arouses bitter discussion, the most ancient surviving books on profane music date to a period prior to Buddhism, meaning earlier than the 5th century BCE, and relate to a musical system that is not very different from the one we know today.

There is a considerable Sanskrit literature about music, which has not yet been studied. Only about twenty works, mostly secondary and relatively recent, have so far been published. In India's manuscript libraries, I have however discovered about 200 works and have found quotations or references close to one thousand works, some of which will certainly be recovered when the libraries are properly catalogued.

There are furthermore several books in Dravidian languages, and particularly in Tamil, Kannada and Malayalam, on original Dravidian works, of which there are translations in Sanskrit.

Megasthenes, who came to India in 302 BCE, tells us that the Indians were very skilful in dancing and music and that they counted 6000 years from the period when Dionysos (i.e. Śiva) taught them music down to Alexander. This corresponds precisely to the legend we find in the *Purāṇas*, or historical books. Moreover, we possess fragments of theoretical works on music earlier than this, such as those of Dattila, and Koha Nandikeshvara, which indicate an already extremely developed musical theory. Only some cross-checking of

112

texts that I have still not been able to do may one day make it possible to fix certain milestones on India's musical history throughout the period that precedes Buddhism. The related documents in our possession today cannot be dated, our main points of reference being the grammarian Pāṇini, who was a close contemporary of the Buddha, and later on Patañjali, in the 2nd century BCE.

The Three Systems

One fact is certain, however: the musical theory of India owes its beginnings to three different sources that co-existed for a long time, each with its own highly developed theoretical literature. One of these systems originated among the Vedic Ṛṣis and was thus Aryan, another in a very ancient Shaivite and probably Dravidian tradition, while the third, which joined the others at a later period, came from a civilisation in eastern India, and was probably of Munda origin. The three musical systems are moreover always mentioned in the ancient works as having been taught by Bharata, Śiva and Hanumanta, although the Bharata work, which in its current form dates at the earliest back to the 2nd century BCE, is already at a stage where the three systems are mixed together. The mixing up of these three theories, each of which had its own philosophy, mathematics and technique, obscures the great works of the Middle Ages on musical theory, and particularly those of Nanyadeva in the 9th century, Abhinavagupta in the 10th century and Śārṅgadeva in the 12th century.

North and South

Nowadays there is a very precise difference between the music of the north and of the south of India, although in theory both belong to the same system and lay claim to the same ancient works. In actual fact, certain survivals of the ancient systems have crystallised in the form of divergent trends in the unified system. Recently, much has been said about Arabic and Persian influence on the music of northern India. This is not very likely however, for the simple reason that

Persia and Arabia had nothing to contribute to India, which was already at a much higher level.

At the same time, the reforms of Venkata Makhin in the 17th century in southern India certainly reintroduced into its music tendencies belonging to a system that was quite distinct from that of the earlier Sanskrit writers, making certain aspects of the music system of southern India somewhat less "Aryan" than that of the north. An appreciation of the historical value of these reforms would require familiarity — which I do not at all possess — with ancient Tamil works and classical Telugu and Kannada works, jealously guarded by the priestly colleges of certain sects, such as the Vīra Śaivas, for example.

The Śrutis

Before tackling the definition of the Hindu modes, we must spare a thought for the scale of notes on which the modes are constructed.

Since the remotest times, Hindu music uses a set of intervals defined by simple numerical ratios. This has led to a division of the octave into a scale of 66 notes, of which 22, corresponding to the simplest numerical ratios, have an expressive value that is more markedly differentiated, thus forming natural steps on which the notes of the various modes are placed.

Naturally, such intervals are not and cannot be equal. Any equalised or tempered division of the octave, however advantageous it may be for the makers of instruments, is clearly an absurdity from the point of view of the physical sounds, since expression is attenuated and disappears when the accuracy of the simple interval deflects, however slightly.

According to the definitions of Hindu music, some intervals that are very close to each other correspond to very different ideas because they are of a different nature. Such is the case, for example, of the harmonic third and the Pythagorean third, whose difference is only 1 comma, but which are considered as entirely different intervals from the point of view of musical expression (in a moment we shall see that this is not a mere abstraction).

114

This is why the equal temperament as practised theoretically in tuning a piano (I say theoretically, because from a physical point of view it is an unrealisable abstraction) is an absurdity from the point of view of musical language. It may even be considered a dangerous practice, because it is based on a physical deficiency in our ear which does not allow us to distinguish easily an error in pitch of less than a semi-comma, whereas our intellect can easily perceive the difference in the distinct ideas represented by these intervals. Similarly, in language, we sometimes find it somewhat difficult to perceive the slight difference in the pronunciation of a consonant differentiating two words, whereas the words themselves, when perceived, represent ideas that are perfectly clear and independent. Often the context alone tells us whether someone is speaking of *mal* (in the sense of *bien et mal*) or of a *malle* (trunk), or of a *mâle* parrot.*

We should not think of simplifying the language by uniting these distinct words with an intermediate pronunciation. The fact that this has been attempted in music indicates an extraordinary failure to recognise the precise and inevitable meaning of musical intervals.

The Theory of Numbers

Since we are speaking of the intervals that form the harmonic scale, it may be interesting at this point to mention the special relationship that exists between some numerical elements and certain ideas or feelings. Music utilises different kinds of basic numerical ratios, each corresponding to a type of expression. Any additional numerical element modifies the type, adding its own character, and consequently modifies the expression in what is always a rigorously identical manner. Thus, knowing how the numbers on one side correspond to ideas and feelings on the other, a glance at a numerical ratio suffices to say exactly what feeling the corresponding sound ratio will arouse.

---

* These three French words, though designating completely different concepts, are pronounced in an almost similar way (Editor's Note).

This fact is clearly of some psychological interest, since it is thus possible for us to equate some of our ideas and feelings, a possibility that is, moreover, in line with the theory of the nature of numbers in Hindu cosmology.

Notation

The musical notation in the Sāma Veda is probably the most ancient existing musical notation. Throughout the thousands of years of its history, India has several times adapted and improved its notation system. Owing to the very nature of the modal system however, in which attention should never focus on the movement of the melodic figure itself, detailed notation is difficult and also, in fact, quite impracticable. The role of notation is thus to fix the various elements of the mode, its scale, its principal notes, its themes or ornaments. For this purpose, Sanskrit notation, which represents the notes by the first syllable of their name, is more than sufficient. Several systems are nowadays in use however, as far as the notation of rhythm and note lengths are concerned. The Somanātha system dating from the 16th century is a great improvement on the previous system, but has been replaced in northern India by the modern Bhatkhande and Vishnu Digambar systems and in southern India by the system currently adopted by the Madras Music Academy.

Rhythms

The vertical division of the sound scale corresponds to a similar horizontal division in time, which is what constitutes rhythm. Rhythm is essentially a succession of long or short elements that can be subdivided, of a periodic nature. Rhythmic elements formed by the relative position of long or short sounds are common to both poetry and music. Whereas poetry utilises these elements in a rudimentary state however, music can subdivide and elaborate them almost infinitely.

Hindu musical theory thus first establishes all possible elements pertaining to rhythmic ratios, known as *gaṇas*, and then utilises them

116

in increasingly complex 3, 4, 5, 6, up to 19 and 32 times, with all the variations brought about by silences or contra tempos.

The Modes

Theoretically, the number of modes is practically unlimited, since they can be counted by hundreds of thousands, but only a few hundred modes are currently in use. Among these, a certain number of basic modes correspond to the rudimentary divisions of the octave. The mode considered to be unaltered has however changed several times over the centuries. Nowadays, the *Bilāval* gamut, corresponding to the major mode, is the one deemed to be without any alteration.

~16~

POPULAR RELIGIOUS MUSIC
IN THE TWENTIETH CENTURY

What we today call religious music has come down to us through three distinct traditions of different origin : (1) a ritual psalmody, which serves as a vehicle for the transmission of sacred texts; (2) music of a mystical or magical character, used as a medium for contacts with the supernatural world; and (3) a musical aestheticism which, taking its inspiration from profane art, tries to integrate the ecclesiastical with the social order and its cultural priorities.

Sources and Function of Religious Music

When we speak of popular religious music [1], we do not refer to inferior or less technically developed forms, but simply to music that is common to the population as a whole, as an audience not only more or less aesthetically motivated, but also involved and eventually participating in the rites.

---

[1] In this essay I have intentionally omitted the contemporary practice of using profane art in churches as a means of attracting a certain audience and of appearing fashionable, for the principles behind this use of music are neither spontaneous nor popular. I refer especially to jazz masses and to the efforts of certain Asian and African countries to create a church music with local colour. Neither have I mentioned the theatre as an instrument of religious education or propaganda, whether representations based on the Rāmāyaṇa or the Mahābhārata in Indonesia, Malaysia and India, the Tazie in Iran, the medieval mysteries of the Oberammergau Passion, or Jesus Christ Superstar. As interesting as these may be, they constitute a different type of religious manifestation from that dealt with here, requiring different historical and psychological approaches. That these spectacles are considered more or less orthodox, or heretical, dissenting, anathema or iconoclastic, does not really change their propagandistic nature.

Until fairly recently, and in many cases to this day, the bulk of knowledge possessed by human groups, tribes, and peoples was transmitted through sung narratives. The legends of gods and heroes, the people's history, as well as invocations, rituals and social laws were preserved for thousands of years by the prodigious memory of bards who transmitted them from generation to generation, of which a written transcription can only record a given moment. This is the case both of the *Iliad* and of the *Vedas*.

Psalms, or sung narratives, constitute a priestly art, a noble art, through which the whole mythological tradition, the ethical and social history is maintained, stored in the memory of the "learned" as long as the oral tradition subsists.

Oral tradition is remarkably stable and unchanging, since it is transmitted by memories which record every detail of style and ornamentation, of movement, rhythm, and modal colouring, etc., while written art is reinterpreted by each generation, and its character quickly degenerates.

In Africa and India there still exists a vast amount of these religious, mystical, historical poems, transmitted by oral tradition, which have never been transcribed and which continue to embody the sum of knowledge and culture, ethics, dogma and laws for a considerable part of mankind.

Among the forms of chanted poetry mainly transmitted through oral tradition, we must mention — above all for their musical interest — the Vedic chants, especially the ones used during the imposing ceremonies called *yajñas*, at which as many as several hundred Brahmins gather around fires dug into the ground, and pour their offerings into the flames. There is also the chanting of the Koran, which is the only musical form officially admitted in orthodox Islam.

At the major Buddhist ceremonies in Southeast Asia and Japan, choirs of monks gather to chant the whole liturgy. In Tibetan Buddhism, these songs are interrupted by the powerful sounds of long brass trumpets and the rolling of drums.

The search for mystical experience, for contact with supernatural forces, for exaltation, for ecstasy and prophetic states, which are the deepest expression of religious feeling, have survived at all times in popular music, despite official religious disapproval.

"Among all the forms of popular poetry, religious poems are the most closely integrated with the life of the people... the planting, the harvests, the gathering of olives or nuts cannot take place without being accompanied by traditional religious songs which transform rural activities into solemn rituals." [2] Certain musical forms have a psycho-physiological effect which help to bring about an awareness of the invisible world of spirits and supernatural forces with which participants may communicate through trances, mystical exaltation, prophetic visions and magical intervention, attaining levels of ecstasy, oblivious to the contingencies of life. This is probably the original and fundamental meaning of the language of music, the language of the gods, in opposition to the spoken language of men. At this level, the religions of the world differ little: the names of their deities may vary, but the reality of perceiving the supernatural, the world beyond, is the same. There is little difference in the semiological significance of an African priest-sorcerer's incantation and a *Bhajana* of the wandering poetess Mirabai, and even of certain of Cesar Franck's compositions, despite the difference in musical form. All contain the same aspiration towards an imminent supernatural state which, by a simplification that seems somewhat naïve in the light of mystical experience, we call God.

The Dionysiac and Animist Tradition

This form of experiential and intuitive religion, based on a perception of the supernatural, embraces all types of mystical, animistic, Yogic or Dionysian experience. Only in the animist religions can we find what might be termed "total" religion, in which every act of life has a religious and magical content. It seems that most official religions were organized in order to eliminate the supernatural form of daily life and to restrict the domains in which the divine presence is

---

[2] P. Toschi, *La Poesia popolare religiosa in Italia* (Roma, 1932), p. 2.

manifest as a constant reality. This leads to Sunday religions, the ethics of which concern only certain actions of life. This transformation has, however, never been totally accepted, and interest in signs and auguries attests to the survival of a deeply rooted animist propensity. The importance attributed to a cat crossing the road, or the bad omen of seeing a priest while coming out of a house, in India as well as in southern Europe, can have a much more determining effect on a person's activities than his going to mass once a week. It is a fact that the latent vestiges of animist beliefs are, in all people, extremely permanent, and explains their periodic reappearance.

The fullest conception of the role of music and dance as a means of communication with the invisible world, of "participation" in the supernatural, seems to have received its greatest philosophical elaboration in a religion, extending from India to the Mediterranean and to Africa, which can be traced back to Protohistory. It is linked to the worship of Śiva in India, of Dionysos or Bacchus in the West, or Osiris in Egypt.

The refusal to separate mind from body in an effort to pierce the mysteries of the world is essentially expressed in the harmony of song and rhythm, in the use of physical actions and erotic relations as taught by Hindu and Tibetan *tantrism*, and in the sublimation of sexual forces as in Yoga, as a means of establishing contact with transcendental values. For Hindu Shivaism, the source of Yoga techniques, man is merely the bearer of his reproductive organs. He is entirely conditioned to the transmission of life, and it is life that gives meaning to the act of creation, which is the macrocosmic aspect of procreation and is essentially of the same nature. It is often through his erotic nature that man is able to lift himself above material appearances and rediscover a relationship with the supernatural and divine world. Songs and dances are an essential means for such contacts, for they imply a total involvement of the physical and intellectual being, life itself being essentially linked to rhythms and pulsations, to spatial and temporal dimensions.

What we know of Dionysian hymns and dances from the descriptions of Greek authors applies, down to the smallest detail, to

121

some of the current forms of song and dance in the cult of Śiva in India, as well as in some of the mystical cults of the Islamic world, in Iran, Turkey, Egypt, and the Maghreb.

The Dionysian dithyramb is the exact counterpart of the Indian *kīrtana* (song of glory), with its hymns and ecstatic dances. The words *bacchos, bacchoi*, which have no known Greek root[3] are equivalent to the Hindu word *bhakta* (participant) and carry the same connotation of inspired madness. The words refer both to the god and to his disciples, as in India today. The *bhajana* (participation), which is the fundamental Hindu religious song, corresponds to the bacchanalia which led to a mystical inebriation, to the "mania" of the bacchants. Christian canticles represent a degenerate and faded form of the *bhajana*.

The northern *bhajana*, and the *Tevaram* of southern India are mystical songs accompanied by an extraordinary elevation of mind and purity of religious feeling. The *bhajana* can easily become a way of life, and not infrequently the best *bhajana* singers become wandering monks who sing the glory of the gods on the outskirts of villages.

In the *kīrtanas* of Bengal, chanted hymns alternate with ecstatic dance, which leads to mystical inebriation.

Dionysus is associated with springtime, and phallic symbols are displayed in his processions. In India, during the spring festival (Holī), Śiva is paraded naked on an ass surrounded by his disciples who sing, dance, and carry phallic symbols, just as in the triumphal processions of Dionysus. A survival of these spring festivals with their character of erotic and sacred frenzy can today be witnessed at carnivals.

The mountain where Śiva dwells is called Nysa. Dionysus is the "God of Nysa", and it is for this reason that the companions of Alexander worshipped him there when they reached that sacred mountain, not far from the modern city of Peshawar.

"Dionysus was probably not a bull god, as has sometimes been presumed, although he is frequently manifested in that form."[4] The Bull is also the vehicle of Śiva and of Osiris. The sacrifice of a bull, or

---

[3] H. Jeanmaire, *Dionysus, Histoire du culte de Bacchus*, Paris, Payot, 1951, p. 58.

[4] H. Jeanmaire, *Dionysus...*, p. 45.

of a cow among the Greeks, was part of the Dionysian ritual. "In a ritual recorded by Pausanias... a bull is the victim which, designated by an inspiration from Dionysus, is seized by men who have anointed their bodies with oil and fat... it was a sort of *corrida* which evokes a similarity with certain Minoan games."[5] The stimulating character which surrounds Spanish bull-fights certainly seems to have been carried over from these ceremonies. There are still many forms of music deriving from Dionysian songs all over the Iberian peninsula, especially those used during processions at the cathedral of Seville.

Outside the limited chants derived from the Hebrew liturgy and the chanting of the Koran, neither the first Christians nor the Mohammedans conceived of music as a part of their rituals. Both religions were anti-Dionysian, and the magical and mystical customs introduced at a later date were originally often the object of persecution. Certain legendary narrations of the Dionysian cycle have nevertheless become part of Christian mythology, such as the transformation of water into wine, walking on the sea, the worship of the bambino, Dionysus as a child. Music of a mystical character was undoubtedly re-introduced into the early Christian church through community gatherings which adapted old songs to new concepts, in much the same way as Negro spirituals appeared in America: mystical, hypnotic songs which, in their African forms, are quite similar to Dionysian chants.

Mystical songs and rituals, adapted to the external forms of new religions, have preserved their character at the popular levels of society in Mediterranean countries.

We must mention the "epidemics of convulsive dances recorded with striking descriptions by mediaeval chroniclers, which in the 14th century took hold of the collective enthusiasm of populations from the Rhine region and Flanders. The dances which accompanied these Dionysian practices in that historical period attest to the persistence... of religious choreography".[6]

---

[5] H. Jeanmaire, *Dionysus...*, p. 259.

[6] H. Jeanmaire, *Dionysus...*, p. 85.

In eastern Thrace, the Dionysian rites of the Nestenarides, associated with Saint Constantine, have survived into the 20th century.
The Nestenarides are the adepts of a sect which, while considered
heretical, is feared and respected. During the festivals of Saint
Constantine, processions lead to the holy place, a sacred fountain, in
each village. After devotions in front of the fountain and a meal in
which the sacrificed lambs are eaten, orgiastic dances take place. "Men
and women, arms stretched out horizontally, begin to dance... swing-
ing from left to right. Soon, the Nestenarides who have entered a
trance move more rapidly, and they furiously seize the icons of Saint
Constantine with both hands, lifting them above their heads and
back down. Then, rushing amidst the dancers, brandishing the icons,
they create disorder... Beside themselves, the Nestenarides suddenly
run off, and like birds, cross hills, forests, ravines and cliffs returning
each to his own village". [7]

Just like the Africans, "the Haitians express their deepest emotions through music. In the songs and dances of the Voodoo service,
music has preserved its variety and its power... The rhythm of the
sacred drums possesses a hypnotic force which augments the mystical
quality of the songs... At times, a possessed person falls into a trance
and is forced by the *loa* (deity) which has mounted him to sing words
that he does not understand. This is called 'the language' in Haiti...
Voodoo also consists of choruses in which they sing and pray, and in
dances which came down from the beginnings of time". [8]

Like all peoples, "it is through music and dance that the (American) Indians worship the gods. With song and dance they obtain the
favour of the Spirits". [9] The same applies to the Macumba of Rio, the
Candombles of Bahia in Brazil, the Obeah of Jamaica.

This trend has again reappeared in the western world by way of
the Africans and of Voodoo, a body of beliefs and rites that crossed
from Africa to the New World with its ecstatic songs and dances.

---

[7] C.A. Romaios, *Cultes populaires de la Thrace*, Athenes, 1949, pp.19-20.

[8] L. Boulton, *Encyclopédie des musiques sacrées*, Paris, Ed.Labergerie, 1969, p.112

[9] L. Boulton, *Encyclopédie...*, p.117.

Voodoo has greatly influenced Negro spirituals and, indirectly, jazz, as well as the modern conception of dance, not so much in its technique as in the inner attitude of its participants.

The ceremonies of song and dance in the churches of Black Americans with their public confessions and their climate of sacred intoxication are a continuation of such rites. A *Gospel Singer*, even sophisticated ones like Mahalia Jackson, is not a product of the Roman liturgy, but a revival in the Christian world of the Afro-Dionysian tradition, a phenomenon that we find periodically in all religions and at all epochs. Such is the case of Tibetan Buddhism, as well as of the mystical sects that have appeared from time to time in the Christian and Islamic worlds. Even among the Greeks, it was assumed that the Dionysian rites were imposed on a well-ordered and, in fact, secularised religion, whereas they represented a return to a far older and deeper religious conception that had remained alive at popular level.

Throughout the Indo-Mediterranean world, whose music is characterized by a modal system conducive to ecstatic states, the Dionysian tradition, which has always belonged to the people, has survived in more or less secret rituals which reappear periodically in one form or another. The Iranian *Dhekr* (remembrance) can hardly be distinguished from the Bengali *Kīrtana*, and we find parallel ceremonies throughout North Africa, among the Aissaouas tribes, as also among the Thaifas of Morocco.

The Islamic world had often been hostile to music, deemed to be a profane and immoral occupation. It is usual to attribute to Mohammed the saying, "May God condemn the beard above which there is a flute". Sacred music is generally limited to chanted recitation of the Koran or the call to prayer. Mystical music found shelter among monastic sects or popular fraternities, where ecstatic dances and erotico-mystical songs are practiced.

In the 13th century, Mevlevi Djelaleddin Rumi founded the fraternity of Mevlevi dervishes who practise the *Dhekr*, bringing together in the Islamic world the remnants of Zoroastrianism, Manichaeism, Nestorianism and Buddhism.

The *Dhekr* of dervishes in the Middle East, especially in Iran, consists of secret ceremonies, open only to the initiated, involving songs based on beautiful religious texts and rhythmic dances, which lead to states of inebriation, unconsciousness and ecstasy. The participants emerge as if transformed by an inner vision, detached from all material cares. Many cultured Iranians end their lives in Dervish monasteries.

Mystical music is an essential element of the Sufi method. It assists man in his spiritual evolution; its call creates an inward inclination of the mind which may, or may not, materialise in dance.

The great moral value of these rites is demonstrated by the Iranian or Arab Sufis, who intone recitations accompanied by dances that cause prophetic trances. The dervishes (religious or civilian) who practise *Dhekr* become models of selflessness, tolerance and saintliness.

"Here we meet with a Manichaeist concept according to which music is considered as an abstract enjoyment for the soul detached from the senses and all worldly effects, and undoubtedly even a means of purification which contributes to that detachment." [10]

In one of his epistles, Mani (3rd century CE) speaks of the "admirable effectiveness, the wonderful power of religious music".

Profane Music and Liturgy

Profane music as an element of the liturgy is a professional art whose participants are as a rule laymen. This conception of music, just as — for that matter — the concept of the architectural arts in the service of the Church to embellish the temple, appears relatively late in the history of mankind, and only when religion becomes an element in the political structures of the state, one of its instruments of expansion and a symbol of its power. Such a situation implies a rigid, dogmatic doctrine, contrary to the original idea of animist or mystical religions which, seeking contacts with the supernatural world

---

[10] H.C. Pucch, *Encyclopédie...*, p. 355.

and faced with the unpredictability of divine favour, could not without sacrilege risk codifying the laws, intentions, and the will of the gods.

In the Christian world, the movement towards aestheticism since the Renaissance has brought a great range of profane music into the church: choral works, organ music, the great masses written by various composers. Moreover, there has long been a tendency to transcribe and codify the poetic-mystical inspiration of individual singers, fixing and thereby transforming mystical music into an impersonal art, as in the case of Gregorian chant.

The expansion of polyphonic music and especially of written music, considered as the essential form of learned music, consigned everything else to a kind of wasteland thought to be of popular origin. In the western world, the "literate" art of those who used writing was considered as a more learned and sophisticated art than the oral tradition. If such a conception is wrong in the case of dance, sculpture and painting, it is certainly misleading for music as well, since an extremely important part of music cannot be written down. It is this very part, often the most difficult and refined in terms of the psycho-physiological effects of the sounds and their communicative value, which tends to disappear in written forms.

Oral and Written Tradition

The belief that music must be approached through its written medium has led to modern methods of studying so-called popular music. The use of transcriptions opens the way to confusion and error since the most elaborate elements are precisely those that cannot be transcribed, or which would require an utterly impractical and complicated notation.

Through an incongruous distortion of our superstition about the written language, we hear musicologists affirm that nothing is known about Byzantine and pre-Byzantine music. It does survive however in certain countries, just as it was in the 7th or the 9th centuries, and we have only to open our ears to recognize it and to identify its Armenian, Syrian, Greek or Roman sources, still alive in existing forms of music in our own times. An illusory concept of history as a merely written record would have us believe that the cultures of the past are truly dead, whereas in many cases they have survived vigorously throughout the ages with hardly any change. We, however, refuse to recognize them, since we persist in classifying as folklore whatever has not been reduced to what can be transmitted by writing.

The improvised poly-vocal songs of Georgia, an almost unique carry-over from ancient polyphonic songs, are classified as folklore, whereas similar but simplified and faded forms, which lost their modal quality in the 16th century Italian transcriptions, are considered, without the slightest musical justification, as a noble and sophisticated art.

For anyone with a musical sense, it is quite evident that the musical quality, the subtlety of form and expressive value of these Georgian polyphonic songs improvised by traditional musicians are far superior to those transcribed and learned from musical notation. Written music becomes old fashioned and loses its style, while music of the oral tradition remains fresh and actual without needing to change. With modern recording techniques we have more opportunities to listen to such forms of music than in the past. [11] We can also develop new methods of analysis, and — more especially — can establish elements of comparison, opening a radically different perspective on the history of religious music. Such means can be used to evaluate the origins of various traditions, which prove to be far older than has often been thought. Far from being the spontaneous creations of an ill-defined entity that we call the "people", they are actually the remains of an elaborate sacerdotal art belonging to civilisations and cultures that have been more or less voluntarily forgotten. "They are the expression of superstitions, rites and beliefs reflecting aspects of a pre-Christian religious environment, more wonderful, more awesome and violent, more pagan" [12] than official religious art.

---

[11] See selected discography below.

[12] P. Toschi, *La Poesia popolare religiosa ...*, p. 2.

Popular religious music in the 20th century, wherever it has not been replaced by profane music, eroded by conventional ecclesiastical art, or supplanted by some dubious and artificial reconstruction such as Gregorian chant, is present in a variety of forms, the remains of ancient cultures and religions. The Celtic, Iberian and Hellenic worlds, Byzantium, Persia, Carthage, India, Turkey, Ethiopia, Mali, North Africa have all preserved in their popular religious music some beautiful examples of a musical art which received its fullest expression in the Dionysian tradition. We must learn how to recognise this tradition in its present forms.

In the Christian tradition, the most impressive ceremonies are the Assyro-Chaldean liturgies of the Middle East, which are among the most admirable remains of pre-Byzantine musical art; those of the Coptic churches of Ethiopia, derived from Hebraic traditions; and the Byzantine rites on Cyprus. We must also mention the chanted hymns of the Armenian, Russian, or Greek church; the archaic songs of churches in Calabria and Sardinia, and the hymns heard in Celtic regions.

The tradition of Byzantine songs, from which Gregorian chant issued in Western Europe, was profoundly altered by the notation of theoreticians who reduced it to extremely simple forms. It lost a good deal of its character, especially the modal consciousness supporting the emotional context, which makes improvisation possible, the modal form subsisting only as a system of classification. Nevertheless, given the superstition about writing in European countries, Gregorian chant is considered a noble art, while non-written variations also deriving from Byzantine chant, which often are actually more elaborate and sophisticated, are considered popular forms.

* * *

In all the societies that we term primitive, dance and music help man to create zones of security, to drive away evil spirits, and to come into contact with supernatural forces. The imminent presence of the supernatural is again progressively becoming part of modern man's subconscious. We feel closer to mystical ecstasy in certain clubs where the young dance than in the coldness of churches. This must be mentioned, since experience that is close to us, even if often instinctive and superficial, allows us to understand what music and dance represent for Asian and African civilisations, with which we have more contact today than in the past. In these contexts, music is no folk survival, but a profound influence, slowly rediscovering its spiritualising and pacifying role in a world doomed to destruction.

According to the Shivaite historical works, the *Purāṇas*, only such a revival can re-establish the equilibrium of mankind during periods of trouble and disorder. The reappearance in our times of the Dionysian spirit, forever latent in the soul of the people, the barely conscious and seldom motivated manifestations of which we can observe on every continent, is Africa and Asia's tremendous contribution to the modern world, and perhaps the only encouraging sign for the future of humanity.

Under the symbol of Śiva, of Dionysus and his cult, ignoring all the notions of hierarchy, caste and race, universal bacchanalia can be organised, an image of the primeval tempest that gave birth to the Universe, bringing about a true fraternity of mankind, beyond dogma, law, ethics and those centres of egotistical interest we call nations. Sacred music is the magical language which, today as in the past and in the future, will allow the majority of the earth's population to communicate with the mysterious world of spirits, attracting their benevolence, and hence, serenity, wisdom and peace.

(Translated from the French by M.F. Metraux)

~17~

THE TRAINING OF PROFESSIONAL MUSICIANS

When talking about musical education, we can easily confuse very different things. The training of professional performers and creative musicians is, in its methods and aims, quite different from the aspects of technical knowledge considered to be useful in general education. Training the ear of children and adults for the purpose of what is sometimes called "musical appreciation" is something else again.

The teaching methods developed in Europe between the 17th and 19th centuries, based on what may be termed "the superstition of writing", have been swept away by modern psychological discoveries. Research into the functioning of the brain — and the memory in particular — have revolutionised the teaching of languages. Music, as always, lags behind in this field. We are still attempting to transcribe complex musical forms in a notation system that is entirely inadequate and are neglecting the essential. We are still employing rudimentary procedures to analyse musical grammar, although we know that ideas, whether belonging to spoken or musical language, are indivisible. We still teach children — and, alas, adults too — to reproduce exactly what was originally written down very inexactly, and this clearly without understanding its meaning. It leads us to tolerate, even from professional performers, a cold, abstract rendering, devoid of meaning. It also leads to the development of a conception of music that no longer considers the musical art as a language with the primary objective of expressing feelings and subtle emotions, but as a form of abstract sound architecture, whose aesthetic content varies according to fashion.

131

Viewed from this perspective, the teaching methods employed in civilisations for whom music has remained essentially a means of communication, of expressing and arousing emotional response, are of fundamental interest and, from a certain standpoint, appear to be much more "modern" than the pseudo-scientific methods based on transcription and analysis. The difference in these methods can be illustrated more or less by a comparison with language. Does one learn a language as children do, by hearing it spoken and trying to imitate its complex structures right from the start, or must one struggle over meaningless grammatical forms, to which we never give a thought in our own speech? Does one become a poet by loving poetry and seeking to utilise its rhythms to express one's feelings, or must one study Greek metrics and attempt to find words to fill them?

Semantics and modern psychology provide us with a formal answer. Taken as a whole, our faculties and senses form an essentially utilitarian instrument for communication, defence and survival, which only function properly when the form and content of our perceptions are synchronised. Our perception of the sound forms of an unknown language, although mechanically equivalent to those of a known language, is in fact very rudimentary and is rapidly ignored by our hearing mechanism. When we are aware of the extremely fine nuances of accent, accentuation and shades of meaning, we understand the content of the language. This phenomenon has sometimes led western musicologists to talk about micro-intervals and imperceptible nuances in oriental music when speaking about forms that are perfectly clear and defined and as distinct as the phenomena of spoken language, which no one dreams of confusing.

One of the most pernicious terms inherited from last century is the word "scientific", applied to simplistic methods of analysis as opposed to proven traditional methods. The fact that the learning of some of the world's greatest civilisations is not expressed in the inadequate and often outdated terminology of a western musicology that is still in its infancy does not mean that it is not a more precise and profound analysis of music and of the audio-mental phenomenon of sound perception. Indeed, it is sometimes far in advance of ours from the point of view of musical science. To be valid, all musical education must take into account the basic principles peculiar to each system, and in most cases, these principles are not interchangeable.

As far as musical education and the training of musicians are concerned, we continue to find two opposing methods. One is an analytical and progressive initiation in the elements of a particular musical system, while the other consists of direct exposure to the most perfect form of the work of art and a progressive effort to comprehend, assimilate and imitate. These different approaches apply equally to the study and understanding of indigenous music in every part of the world as they do to the widening of our musical horizon by an understanding of other cultures. The direct method is the one that is considered to be the most effective today in the teaching of languages, and it is the one that has always been employed in all eastern countries for the teaching of music. Nowadays, it is the only method in the west for training jazz musicians, who have taught us to rediscover a feeling for rhythm and for improvised development, destroyed by the writing down of music and its teaching.

It is thanks to this direct teaching method that the music of the Middle East and India has reached such a richness of intervals, such rhythmic complexity, such a variety of attack and embellishment, and above all such unity of musical form and meaning, bringing about prodigious developments in musical art in a direction wholly unknown in the western world.

The concept of teaching by direct contact with music at its highest technical and artistic level is far more modern than the ones still too often used in schools of the European kind. It is incredible to see so-called modern schools springing up on all sides, claiming to adapt European methods — said to be, for heaven knows what reason, more "scientific" — to the teaching of music in eastern countries. As might have been expected, such schools have produced disastrous results in every country of the East and Africa that have attempted to teach music according to western methods.

Musical taste is formed by listening to a musician, not to a schoolmaster. Nowadays, records play a fundamental role in this. The radio, unfortunately, has so far been rarely aware of its educational role.

To train a professional musician, the only formula that appears to be adequate is the permanent and personal relationship of teacher and pupil. Whatever theories they may hold, the great musicians of the west, like all the others, always end by saying "I am a pupil of Enesco", or "I am a pupil of Cortot or Lipati", because it is only through such personal contact with great masters that they have been able to perfect their art.

In the Middle East, in Iran and India, the handing down of great musical art has always required this permanent contact of the apprentice musician with a master. A musician will gather around him a few gifted pupils who listen while he practises, are there when he plays for his own pleasure, or when he gives a concert, asking questions, trying to assimilate his style and imitate his creative imagination, gradually grasping the secrets of his trade and art.

In musical forms where the creative element and the technical element are equally important, nothing can replace this method of teaching. Those responsible for music education in the Middle East should make a serious examination of their conscience. If efforts continue to focus on collective, sterile teaching, on choral and instrumental ensembles which — despite the resulting sound volume — reduce music to a vague prefabricated skeleton, a nebulous folklore stripped of all the subtle elements that constitute a noble and refined art, then one of the most profound and most human musical arts will cease to exist. The training of professional musicians to the highest level is the only way for musical art to survive. The solution lies in discovering the means to enable the great musicians of the present day to train qualified pupils according to the ancient and proven method of communal living. This problem is neither very difficult nor very costly to solve. Having made the same mistakes as other countries, India alone today seems to be taking the necessary measures to save its musical heritage by returning to traditional teaching methods with State support. In this sense, it is a forerunner among eastern countries and is gradually reclaiming its rightful place in world

134

culture. This cannot be done without effort and courage, because it means a gradual elimination of the so-called conservatoires, choirs, "oriental orchestras" and other formulas invented because their names sounded right at international gatherings, but whose principles were unfortunately not applicable to modal music and to its preservation as one of the highest — and perhaps the very highest — forms of musical art.

Iran, too, is making a first move towards the rehabilitation of traditional master-pupil teaching. If it continues, Iran should be able to reclaim its place as one of the great musical cultures of the world, instead of becoming, like so many other countries, one of the West's musical suburbs.

In a country whose culture is under threat, as is the case of all the autonomous civilisations of the Middle East, the first problem is not diffusion, but — as they say in the Soviet Union — "executive training", which for music means the training of young musicians capable of maintaining the national classical art at its highest level. To achieve this, experience everywhere shows that there is no other method than the traditional one, which requires the communal life of master and a few pupils, because in the musical art of Iran or India, music and musicians form a single entity. Music disappears with its last qualified representative. It is therefore necessary and logical to regard the musician who bears the responsibility for preserving the musical art of a particular civilisation as a "living national treasure", as in Japan. People who lose their language and their music cease to exist as a cultural and national entity and have no further contribution to make to world culture.

135

~18~

IMPROVISATION

The difficulty experienced by contemporary western musicians in defining and understanding the term "improvisation" is highly indicative of the evolution of musical concepts.

Improvisation is simply the ease with which the development of an idea is expressed. This is only possible insofar as music is a language conveying thoughts and feelings and does so with the formulas of a definite language with precise rules of grammar.

Improvisation is as natural as the spoken word, and the musician develops the musical idea with greater or lesser elegance of phrasing, greater or lesser subtlety of expression or strength of conviction, according to the quality of his training and individual talent.

A prelude by Chopin, a piece by Liszt, or a melody of Schubert's are often notated improvisations. At his piano, the musician follows an emotional or descriptive idea and develops a melodic form within a very definite pattern. He develops the idea in different ways using the same or other formulas. Anyone taking up the *Claire de Lune* pattern from "Werther" on the piano can spin it out indefinitely. Between the lines of Liszt's scores, the patterns of gypsy improvisation can be heard.

There is no doubt that up to the 19th century, performers would wait impatiently for the cadenza, which would give them the opportunity to throw a fireworks display around the theme, just as their imagination took them, but without abandoning the feeling of the work, its style, mode, flow, or basic patterns.

Improvisation follows a similar process in other musical systems. In order to improvise, the musician must have something to say, an emotive and sentimental theme, as well as very precise grammar, and an unerring logic of patterns ready to hand. As a mental process, the development of an Indian *rāga* is in no way different from a speech or a sermon in which the speaker seeks to express a guiding theme by means of coherent grammar and carefully prepared effects.

Without the force of the thematic and emotional idea, without the strict framework of the modal scale, the fixed patterns, the nuances of attack and the embellishments enhancing expression, improvisation is impossible.

It is probably the excessive freedom in sound ratios and the absence of formulas that make some contemporary musicians believe that improvisation is governed by an element of chance. Precisely the opposite is true. A speaker employing words at random without the logical link provided by the expression of clearly-formed thoughts in a strictly established conventional linguistic formula would be booed by his audience and would soon run out of ideas. Exactly the same occurs in musical improvisation, the result of long practice and absolute mastery of the formulas of a precise language.

We have no other means of communication than the formulas of language. We recognise the value of a language by the richness of its vocabulary and the complexity of its grammatical conventions. Music is no different. To believe that music can be a means of communication beyond conventional, classical language — which can certainly be extended and modified, but not ignored — is merely a childish and barren dream. The freedom thus acquired destroys that most important instrument of expression that language, whether musical or spoken, represents for mankind. The possibilities of free discourse and improvisation are eternally bound by the conventions of language.

~19~

BASIC ELEMENTS
IN THE VOCABULARY OF SOUND

Like language, music belongs to a system of communication between one individual who thinks, conceives and feels emotions and transmits them to other individuals through the means of sound. No one can know what another being is feeling or thinking unless these emotions, sensations or ideas are reduced to more or less symbolic formulas, which allow an external summary to be transmitted to another living being. The recipient must know the key to interpret these symbols and, by inference, compare them to his own feelings and experiences, certain elements of which he then attributes to the person who has sent the message. We thus obtain a kind of mental diagram of someone else's emotions, and attribute a value to it, naturally assuming that the facts experienced are similar and comparable in both cases.

Through special cases, we know that this is not always so. When someone who is colour-blind sees a tree, we have no way of knowing whether his experience resembles what for us is red or green, or whether it is something else. We also know that the characteristics of our hearing organs vary a great deal. Sensitivity to different frequencies is very unequal, with a different placing of holes in the lyre with eleven thousand strings, as our ear is poetically known. The feeling given by a harmony, by way of example, may vary considerably from one person to another. This may also lead to a highly divergent aesthetic appreciation, which is however equally justifiable.

Recent experiments in the field of perception tend to show that we only perceive ratios, never absolutes. This has been demonstrated in recent work on colour perception. There are no colours, but only ratios that establish themselves at various points of a light spectrum. If this spectrum is extended or shortened, for the same light frequency we perceive colours that vary according to the other regions of the spectrum. The same is true of all our senses, touch (cold or hot), taste, smell and, of course, sound.

At the level of sound, ratios are all that we can perceive analytically, and — as with our other senses — our perception is limited by the differentiation capacity of our receptive organ, the ear, and our perceptive and analytical organ, the brain. This is why, if we wish to establish a coherent theory about the basis of musical art, we must, first of all, carefully study these two aspects of our audio-mental receptive mechanism and determine their limitations and possibilities. Some studies have been carried out on the ear's mechanism, but very few on the cerebral mechanism to which our ear transmits its impressions, which is the real perceptive organ, the ear merely acting as its microphone.

It seems rather curious that, in formulating musical theories, the possibilities and limitations of man's audio-mental system have rarely been taken into account, and scholars often let themselves be drawn into speculations that seem to take no account of these possibilities and limitations, which are instrumental in our appreciation of sound phenomena. Pythagoras is probably one of the first great culprits in this, and we have apparently not yet managed to free ourselves from the mathematic-symbolic-musical lucubrations of the ancient Greeks, whose basis also totally misses the mark of the clearest physiological and psychological facts.

It is easy to observe that the division of articulated sound that we use in practice in our spoken language is not a logical one. It could be improved quite easily using physiological and experimental data. But no one would dream of taking advantage of the defects to remake a purely abstract alphabet, utilising the properties of the golden section, logarithms, or the properties of triangles. However amusing they may be, the minute calculations that can thus be made clearly lead nowhere, since we can neither perceive nor pronounce new vowels and consonants which do not take into account our powers of articulation. For the construction of spoken language, we are forced to do our best with a certain number of phonemes, happily already very numerous, which we group together in various ways.

However, just as we can establish a fairly complete classification of utilisable and differentiable sounds according to the location spots of articulation and the nature of the vocal effort, we should be equally able to establish a musical alphabet based on our powers of sound perception and differentiation. After this, we should find it much easier to establish the bases of musical grammar according to the data of the systems we choose to employ to classify the sound elements.

In reading the lucubrations of Archytas, Aristoxenes, Ptolemy, or the implications of Timaeus, followed by the theories of Avicenna, Farabi, and Boece, to include the most modern theoreticians, it is amazing to see them apply to the observation of musical phenomena geometrical and algebraic theories that may be valid in elementary astronomy and architecture, but have nothing to do with our sound-perception mechanism. Music is provided with a series of intervals with nice numerical forms that we can no more discern than we can see the satellites of Venus or the rings of Saturn with our naked eye.

It must be recognised — and it is to their honour — that in every era musicians have with great obstinacy resisted theoreticians who claim to explain to them what they are doing wrong (as it were), somewhat like grammarians who study our language and establish what they believe to be its laws, then explaining to us that we were wrong to infringe on the laws they have just established on the basis of what we have told them.

Nowadays, unfortunately, we tend to take theories seriously, whether they are political, ethical, metaphysical or scientific. This is why we are no longer wholly at ease with the old and totally inadequate musical theories, since we hesitate to consider theory as an approximation, to be treated in practice lightly and freely, like a senile old lady. It may consequently be very useful for us to revise all the basic data in the vocabulary and morphology of musical languages and check them on an experimental, controllable and indisputable basis.

In fact, through a strange aberration inherited from the Greeks, our theory of the scale, starting from an observation of the proper data on simple ratios, studies this data in the laboratory, following theories based on geometry or algebra, which are totally foreign to it. The result is a "scientific" scale that differs considerably from the one from which we started, which we continue to use surreptitiously in practice whenever we can. This is because an attempt has been made to arrange the elements according to principles that are wholly foreign to them and are not applicable to music, or at least to our audio-mental organs through which we perceive them. The enormity of the practical joke known as equal temperament is clear proof, if any is needed.

As we have already said, we only perceive ratios. In this very special language that we call music, such ratios are first and foremost frequency ratios, to which ratios of intensity and duration are added. What we call sound ratios are as often as not frequency complexes. We shall see that the various musical languages utilise interval ratios, duration ratios or rhythm, intensity ratios (the key in the case of keyboard instruments) and sound ratios in varying degrees.

The first element of our musical vocabulary concerns frequency ratios, which are based on a well-defined audio-mental phenomenon, differently adapted in the morphology of the various musical languages.

Our audio-mental mechanism for perceiving frequency ratios only functions within a certain range of hearing that varies very little and only in the case of certain simple and very definite numerical values. We shall see that some prime numbers play a fundamental and decisive role in establishing such ratios and making them intelligible.

Whenever we represent sound ratios arithmetically, the first thing to avoid is any kind of generalisation, without paying great attention also to the limits of analytical perception of the frequencies. It is because we can easily perceive twice 2 that we conclude that we can perceive twice 4, since we certainly cannot register directly the nature of a shape in which a number such as 2^{13} appears, whereas we can at once perceive the nature of a square or rectangle. At a certain point, there is a limit that has to be determined beforehand. We must therefore, at each step, check experimentally what in theory appears to be a logical sequence.

Rhythm and Scale

In the overall structure of the musical scale, there is no break between the frequency scale and the rhythmic scale. The latter is merely the continuity of the descending melodic scale. This is very important for an understanding of the psycho-physiological effect of organised sound. When the air pulsation slows down, the sound becomes lower and lower down to a limit point (about 16 vibrations per second), from which point our perception of the pulsation becomes rhythmic. This makes a difference to our way of perceiving various frequencies, but is not a natural difference in the vibratory scale itself. The construction of rhythmic formulas, as they appear in music, utilises periodic elements chosen according to a basic beat, just as the notes of the scale correspond to frequencies chosen according to a basic, fundamental or tonic beat. Indeed, it seems probable that the bases of rhythmic beat and pulsation perceived as a sound pitch are as a rule common and that, in the overall balance of the work of art, rhythm and harmony are strictly co-ordinated. As the continuation of each other, they have to remain associated if we are seeking a physiological effect. Rhythmic limits are established like the limits of the scale. Double measures are the equivalent of octaves. Triple time corresponds to fifths, quadruple time to fourths, while times to the power of 5 evoke feelings similar to those produced by thirds. We find the same numerical limitations as in the scale. Rhythmic embellishments have the same character as melodic embellishments.

However, our notion of the time beat seems to be inverse to the beat of the melodic scale. Indeed, we speak of double time for a beat that is two times less frequent, while we consider that an upper octave, i.e. higher pitched, is the double of the octave immediately lower, which it is from the point of view of frequency. This seems to be a convention, however, in as much as the notes we call "high" are termed "low" in certain musical systems, and vice-versa.

In order to determine the whole of the numerical ratios utilised or utilisable in music, we shall look at the scale and first of all the limits of our perceptions, which exclude the utilisation of certain categories of elements.

In practical terms, our ear perceives all sounds, whether simple or compound, with a frequency ranging from 16 to 16 000 vibrations per second. But *perceiving* does not mean analysing, being able to comprehend or utilise the sounds in an intelligible musical language. The sound elements have to be extremely simple and differentiated for our ear to perceive them directly and properly, and for our brain to classify them easily and give them a meaning, an emotional colouring, which may be inherent in the intervals or be conventionally attributed to them.

It is the same for all the other arts. Architecture, for example, is not a confused mass of complex shapes, but a finished design with simple lines, its proportions measured with precision. Only then is it an art that gives us an aesthetic feeling.

We shall see — and this is confirmed by experience — that our ear (just as our eye) only recognises with precision ratios or intervals based on the first four prime numbers (1, 2, 3 and 5), as well as their multiples and coefficients up to a degree inversely proportional to their value. This coefficient seems to be 8 for 2, 5 for 3, and 3 for 5, i.e. 256 for 2 (the coefficient for the Pythagorean limma), 243 for 3 (likewise a limma coefficient) and 125 for 5.

Prime Numbers and Perceptions

The Octave

Strictly speaking, 1 is not a number. It is an undifferentiated basis for all numbers. Multiplied by itself, 1 remains unvaried. Multiplied by other numbers, it identifies with them without transforming them.

The first truly numerical element is 2. It determines the framework within which the differentiation of intervals is constructed. This framework we call the "octave". The name octave, from "eighth sound", is not a useful name in the heptatonic system. It is absurd when used for the Chinese pentatonic, as it is also in the dodecaphonic system.

The octave, double frequency, or the string divided in two, creates for our ear no feeling of true differentiation, but a sort of limit, of frame, in which sounds seem to reproduce without altering their character. The differentiation of intervals, scales, music, is born between the two poles of the octave.

The fundamental dualism represented by the octave is found in all aspects of creation, and particularly in the division of mankind into two complementary constituents, male and female. It is not by chance, but the expression of a law found in all things, that the female voice is an octave above the male. From the point of view of musical expression, intervals that are identical but inverse always belong to the kind expressed in Chinese musical theory by the terms "lower generation" and "upper generation".

The same interval, the fifth for example, produced by lower generation, i.e. starting from the bottom, has an active, enterprising, virile character. When produced by upper generation, i.e. descending the octave, it has a passive, sweet, feminine character. The descending fifth interval is called the fourth. In the sound scale, we always find that the fifth has a masculine character and the fourth a feminine one. The sun is always described in fifths, and moonlight by fourths, heroism by fifths and sweetness and shyness by fourths. The opposing nature of lower and upper generation applies to all intervals.

The frame of development for the scale of intervals is thus rhythmed by number 2, by the succession of octaves. It vanishes from our physical power of hearing at the ninth octave (about 16,000), but from our power of mental discrimination at the seventh octave (about 4096). If we continue the octaves downwards, the pulsation

144

limit perceived as a sound pitch is at about 16 pulsations per second. Beyond this, the pulsations are perceived as rhythmic elements. We shall find the bases of our rhythmic data — always the double of each other — by continuing the octaves in slower and slower frequencies. If we give a hemi-demi-semi-quaver the value of 16 pulsations (almost the double of the practical speed of the trill, which is about 10), we shall have as lower octave (or half value) the demi-semi-quaver (8 per second), then, from octave to octave, the semi-quaver (4 per second), the quaver (2 per second), the crotchet (1 per second), the minim (1 every two seconds), the semibreve (1 every 4 seconds). We consequently have seven octaves forming the basis of the rhythmic elements, corresponding to the seven melodic octaves.

The rhythmic scale is thus the continuation of the melodic scale and has the same characteristics from the emotional point of view.

To be precise, from the point of view of psycho-auditive reactions, we really need a time-measuring system that is different from the hour-minute-second system. The division of the daily cycle into 86,400 seconds is arbitrary and does not correspond to our vital rhythms, which, from the standpoint of the relation between numbers and vital reactions, falsifies our data. For musical theory, the Indians prefer to use the average breathing rhythm. It would however greatly complicate our comparisons if we were to use another time-measuring system to calculate frequencies and we have no need to attain such precision in this brief survey.

It is however useful to recall that for a serious study on man's emotional reactions to frequency ratios, it is most important to calculate them using some sort of unit that is a reality for our organism, and not an arbitrary standard of time measurement. If we were also to consider the reactions of other living beings, such as birds, we should on each occasion take the unit of time measurement appropriate to them. If we wish to transcribe the songs of birds in terms that are comprehensible to us, we must transpose them into another measurement standard — our own — which is much slower. We should then be very surprised to hear that bird conversations often closely resemble our own.

Absolute Pitch

The absolute pitch of sounds, meaning the ear's reaction to frequencies experienced with regard to a given theoretical standard, is a reality of musical experience. It is especially important in systems with abstract tendencies, in which harmonic relations are false and our mind instinctively seeks a consistent and permanent point of reference. Absolute pitch played a role in ancient Chinese music and tends to do so in western music in so far as it is tempered and dodecaphonic, i.e. anti-natural from the point of view of the intervals and their ratios. We can even hear the expressive difference between a piece played in C minor or in B flat minor, a difference that is based above all on mental practice, since we must not forget that our B flat was — in absolute pitch — a C for Bach. We do not know moreover whether we should consider that our mental diapason has changed and whether we perceive Bach's music as it was perceived in its own time, or as if it had been transposed.

The Fifth

As everywhere in nature, differentiation in music appears to us with number 3. This is the number that in music gives rise to the interval which we — rather mistakenly — call the fifth, on the pretext that it is the fifth note in a certain scale that we hardly use any more.

If we follow its multiples as we did for the octave, the fifth gives us a cycle which — this time — is not repetitive in the effect it creates on our hearing mechanism, but causes (for a reason that has not been determined) a difference in the impression it makes on us, the feeling it appears to evoke. This cycle, which is superimposed on the octave cycle, never corresponds with the latter. In the series of octaves, it creates three-sound cycles, then seven-sound, then twelve-sound, and lastly fifty-two sound cycles, and so on. With each cycle a new kind of interval appears, formed with the cycle of octaves. A reverse cycle of descending fifths creates a parallel series, which never merges with the former.

Naturally, the discovery of this little arithmetical game of the cycle of fifths has made theoreticians and other lovers of easy mathematics happy, from Antiquity to our own times. In actual fact, the series of fifths plays no role in music. It is due to a simple coincidence between two systems utilising the prime multiples of three — for different reasons — that it has been considered important. The history of the scale of fifths has been and remains a disaster in the psychological theory of music. The Chinese probably invented it. The Greeks — with childlike enthusiasm — unhesitatingly saw in it the key to the music of the spheres. And we have stupidly followed them, without any reflection. We still use it to tune instruments approximately in another system that has absolutely nothing to do with fifths.

What actually happens is that our ear and brain have an analytical aptitude through which we are immediately able to recognise certain numerical factors, which we experience as direct emotional impressions. For us, a fifth is something recognisable, like red or blue, or like a square or a triangle. The simple ratios of numbers create within us direct impressions that do not require reflection, or pondered mental action, to be interpreted. Without reflecting, we record the shape of a double square or the colours of the Belgian flag. In rather the same way, we perceive a 3×3, i.e. a second, a D, if the base is C — but this is not because the D is the fifth of G. Of course, we use this trick to transpose on our mechanical instruments, or to tune a piano. But that is something different. The fact that the second is a fifth of a fifth is not the reason why it appears to us as an intelligible and precise interval. It so happens, by chance, that in both cases we encounter a 3 multiplied by 3. But this does not imply any direct relationship between the two systems, one mental and the other technical. We may, however, employ the expressions "cycle of fifths", "cycle of thirds", "cycle of octaves", as an easy way of classifying the multiples of 3, 5 or 2.

In fact, owing to the limitations of our possibilities of immediate audio-mental analysis, we shall see that we only perceive the multiples of 3 up to the fifth. This is also why musical systems based exclusively on the coefficients of 3, such as Chinese music, can only be pentatonic. Beyond this limit, we no longer recognise the interval.

We find it indeterminate, because we cannot sing it or play it with any precision. Indeed, we automatically replace it with another neighbouring interval belonging to another cycle, of which we shall now speak.

The indefinite development of the cycle of fifths, amusing and satisfying as it may be, cannot communicate to our perceptive mechanism any sounds that alone play a role in musical language. In submelodic octaves, i.e. rhythms, the 3 gives us the first truly rhythmic base, the first element of movement with a vital character capable of impacting us psychologically. The magical action of sounds begins with the waltz.

Number 4

Number 4 is not a prime number. We shall see that numbers that are not prime numbers play no major role in our cerebral reaction mechanism to music, which immediately breaks numbers into their constituent parts. Four is simply the basis of the double octave. It belongs to a neutral class in which the scale of sounds develops. We may remark however that 8 (i.e. $2^{3)}$ marks a slight differentiation. The sounds of the third octave have a slightly different colouring from those of the other octaves. Both Greek and Iranian theories take this fact into account. The ambitus of the mode is the double octave. In the third octave, the notes change their name and there is a tendency to give them a distinctive character.

Number 5

The highest of the prime numbers that we are able to perceive and recognise immediately is "5". We can only recognise higher numbers if they are symmetrically arranged to form a familiar figure, if, in fact, they are considered as agglomerations of lower numbers.

In our audio-mental mechanism, 5 and its coefficients appear to play a very important role. Naturally, in our nomenclature — which is absurd from the point of view of our numerological cerebral mechanism — the intervals based on 5 are called sixths and thirds.

An independent cycle, the cycle of thirds, based on the number

5, overlaps the octave cycle (cycle of number 2) and the cycle of fifths (cycle of number 3).

5 gives rise to highly remarkable emotional reactions. In music, emotion is expressed by 5. This is probably also true of all our emotional reactions, but our knowledge of the electronics of our own brain is still very poor. When they are related to other intervals, the intervals of the cycle of 5 appear to contribute a degree of sensitivity, of lively reaction. While the cycle of fifths (of the number 3) provides abstract, architectural harmonies, the cycle of thirds moves us, acting directly on our sensitivity. Whenever singers or violinists manage to strike that heart rending note that moves your very soul, if you have the courage to take up your measuring instruments, you will find that the interval they are singing or playing is not tempered and does not even belong to the cycle of fifths, but that the musician has found the coefficient of 5, which alone brings life and emotion into nature as it does to arts. When they manage to manufacture electronic brains employing the coefficient of 5, the brains themselves will probably at once become emotional and independent. For the time being, they are still working on factor 2 and are therefore not dangerous.

We recognise the coefficients of 5 up to the third, whereas we recognise the coefficients of 3 up to the fifth. In practice therefore, there could be no scale of the cycle of 5 because it would only have three notes. Usually, musical scales utilise a mixture of elements from the cycle of 3 and the cycle of 5, as well as elements combining 3 and 5. Thus we obtain the heptatonic scales, scales of nine sounds, and scales of twelve sounds.

Furthermore, the first element of the double cycle of fifths divides the octave into two parts C-F, G-C, which we call — again an unfortunate name — tetrachords. The cycle of 5 is found within the tetrachords, just as the cycle of fifths is found within the octave.

The complete range of intervals of cycles 2, 3 and 5 and their combinations up to the third multiple numbers 52 sounds. It is on this scale that all musical systems without exception are built. Each of these 52 notes has a distinctive expressive character, which is entirely explicable from their structure, forming the basic vocabulary of all music.

There are probably some well-ordered minds among you who believe that western music rigorously uses an equally tempered dodecaphony. I regret that I must shatter your comfortable illusion. Let them first measure the tuning of their piano using an electronic instrument, and I promise them a few surprises. And if they then wish to analyse a record of Charliapin in Boris Godunov, their amazement will know no bounds.

Numbers 7 and 11

To come back to numbers, however, the other prime numbers are not recognisable by our audio-mental mechanism, nor for that matter by our other perceptions. Without counting, we cannot know whether there are 7 or 11 apples in a basket. Similarly, we can neither recognise nor play with any precision the intervals based on 7 or 11.

The first of the interval by 7 is the 7th harmonic (7/4), an interval whose lack of musicality has always demoralised theoreticians. After it come its reverse, the augmented tone (8/7), a little wider than the major tone and totally disagreeable. The next interval by 7 is 7/6, which is more comfortably placed between the unaccented minor third and the second 1/4. Aristoxenes and Ptolemy, trying at all costs to make room for this interval, call it the minim third. Its reverse is a little lower than 1/4. These intervals are wholly outside the range of the scale. We always prefer a near interval, which is more complex in structure, but formed of the coefficients 2, 3 and 5.

It is possible for some individuals endowed with a superior mental mechanism to appreciate intervals by 7, but I have never encountered any. At the same time, this does not mean that the cycles of 7 and 11 may not have a particular psychological effect. However, this lies outside music duly conceived as an intelligible art, rather than as a therapeutic or magical means.

It seems, in fact, that the cycles of 7 and 11 can be utilised with the aid of an artifice, but only in the rhythmic octaves, where they can be broken down into 4 (2 times 2) and 3 and in 3 x 3 + 2, for example. Magical properties have been attributed to them: beneficent for 7, maleficent for 11.

When we envisage the physiological effect of music, there is no absolute demarcation between the emotional effect that we can call artistic and certain sub-intellectual physical reactions, which can be very strong. In dance music, jazz and African music in general, we often find ourselves between the two fields, and sometimes it is important to know the one in order to understand the other. Dance can produce a sort of inebriety and lead to states close to ecstasy. Very precisely determined rhythms play a part in producing such states. Any serious study of musical vocabulary must take into account the absence of any discontinuity between the physiological and the psychological effects of sounds, between their physical properties and their mental interpretation.

Other Scales

The three cycles of 2, 3 and 5 determine the vocabulary of music — of all music. For mankind there is no other series of intelligible intervals. They are not naturally perceived by us as numerical series, but as shades and nuances of feeling, just as we perceive the different colours of the spectrum. We get there by instinct, and all theoreticians of music, in every civilisation, have experimentally observed their principal elements.

It is not easy, however, to measure frequency ratios with the aid of summary instruments, and making a slight mistake and systematising it results in the construction of parallel scales. Such scales may appear logical, but are mere abstractions that can only be used for an approximate representation of musical events, and have to be re-interpreted according to the data of our audio-mental mechanism. Thus, we find among the Greeks, the Arabs, and the Chinese interval values that arise from arithmetic lucubrations that have nothing to do with reality, but on paper they can be used to make diagrams with a wonderful symmetry. The golden segment and the properties of triangles have been sought for sounds. Naturally, any kind of mathematics can be found in music, since the series of harmonics is in theory nothing more than a series of numbers. Music is not, however, limited to the physical phenomenon of resonance. It is an intelligible language, in fact the most intelligible of languages, and in any case, the most direct.

Of the artificial interpretations of the series of sounds, the most remarkable one for us is still tempered dodecaphony, an easy solution to a technical problem that was bothering the manufacturers of keyboard instruments. But may it please Ernest Ansermet, who honoured me with his sarcasm in a recent work giving a solution, says he, to all musical problems, we have no audio-mental mechanism to perceive — and to perceive exclusively — the multiples of $\sqrt{12/2}$, an operation that is rather difficult to do at first sight. Temperament is thus a fiction. We inevitably hear something else, meaning substitute intervals that are more or less approximate. But loss of the meaning of sounds in a system where everything is illogical and approximate has led us to seek other methods than the scale of intervals to establish expressive ratios, a new kind of vocabulary, which could also be a wonderful enrichment, perhaps even the discovery of a wholly new art.

Other Ratio Systems

We thus employ other systems to restore life to piano music. We listen to the scale as little as possible. Using a hearing defence device, we make our ears insensitive to precise intervals. In this we are greatly assisted by the piano's three chords, which are not in unison and create a wonderful cloud of foggy harmonics. Our attention is wholly fixed therefore on volume and tempo values. It is to the weakness of the scale that we owe that marvellous instrument of expression that is the pianist's touch. The value relating to the shock of the hammers on the strings creates a whole new system of sound ratios. It is also and above all the variation of note duration that makes us play a little before or a little after the metronomic tempo, thus establishing a totally new code of ratios with an astonishing delicacy and a remarkable quality of expression.

Another ratio system can be established according to instrumental colouring (or the organ stops), constituted by variable harmonic groups forming true chords. By mixing the groups of sounds formed by the harmonics, polyphony lets us establish a completely different system of sound ratios.

In any case, it would seem to be a good thing that these different ratios could only cause precise emotional reactions if they are established in the framework of the series 2, 3 and 5. Of course, forms of abstract art can always be created independently of audio-mental reactions, but it is difficult to see to what advantage, since the related theoretical possibilities are not better. Furthermore, to the extent that the vocabulary of musical art distances itself from elements that cause emotional reactions, it loses most of its audience, who take refuge in a folklore which, even if inferior in concept and form, is more human in its vocabulary, however simplistic it may be. Certainly, the abstract artist neglects part of his mission.

Musical Morphology and Syntax

The vocabulary of sound is established according to certain laws common to all musical languages, but the vocabulary is fairly vast and each of the various systems only uses a part of it. Moreover, the elements of this vocabulary can be joined to form highly different structures. The development of morphology is often influenced by the nature of the vocabulary that limits its possibilities and changes its tendency.

Modal Music

It appears that basic morphology, which is in any case the most widespread form of musical language originally, is the form that we may call modal in the Greek and oriental meaning of the term, in which the various sound ratios are established by their relation to a fixed and permanent note. This system makes it possible to use very varied and very nuanced interval forms. With a certain amount of practice, since frequency and interval are identified with each other, a sound pitch can be immediately associated with the particular ex-

153

pression of an interval. This means that a sound is at once associated with an idea, an expression, as is the case for words in spoken language. This identification even takes place when the intervals occur in rapid succession. With this system, it is thus possible to construct phrases of great complexity, express rich, varied and subtle nuances of feeling. This musical form's morphology is closest to the languages spoken in the West and is therefore probably the most easily assimilated by our brain, whose mechanism is so conditioned by speech that we sometimes even confuse it with thought.

The Melodic Aspect

The melodic aspect, in which the ratios establish themselves in succession and where the tonal basis can be varied, is only an ornamental aspect of musical structures, never a basic, as it is sometimes made to appear. To have a meaning, melody requires an underlying system of reference. In any popular song of the Indo-European world, this system of reference is almost always modal, even when it remains unexpressed and almost unconscious. This is what harmonists seem not to understand, when they use popular themes and change their meaning by placing them in a modulating or atonal system. What they do to the theme is what for us might be the use of an English word or set of words if we were to give them a meaning according to their sound in French. In rhythmic octaves, the rhythmic mode establishes itself by means of a formula applied rigorously on a given beat. It is the same for a good jazz rhythm.

The Modulant

In modulatory systems, such as Chinese music, the limited sound groups are established on a base, as in modal morphology, but the base shifts, forming new groups. In this way, the same note can have different meanings, since the base that determines its value has changed. This is also the same as in what we call modulation in western music. The melodic subtlety of modulating systems decreases with the increase in frequency. It means, in effect, re-establishing a scale of values with each variation of the tonal base, in order to give the sounds meaning. However, the impression created by the change in meaning of an immobile note is a new means of expression that is slow, with little variation, but is powerful.

In rhythmic octaves, modulation is represented by changes in the beat values, linked to each other by simple ratios. It is thus possible to establish aesthetic variations in the divisions of tempo, but this causes the rhythm to lose its vital character, its psycho-physiological effect. All western classical music is constructed like Chinese music on modulating rhythms, i.e. variable divisions of the tempo, which we appreciate intellectually, although they have no direct impact on our nervous or motor system. The whole magical or intoxicating effect of music is suppressed by rhythmic modulation.

Harmonic and Polyphonic

Expressive sounds may in certain cases be perceived simultaneously. Their individual meaning remains recognisable if they are organised in certain simple forms, and a kind of expressive resultant is achieved. The degree of complexity of sounds for which we can clearly establish an intelligible resultant increases considerably if the ear is trained. This is why no real demarcation can be established between concordance and dissonance in chords with a difference of degree and not of nature. The problem of simultaneous sounds is complicated by purely physical accessory phenomena, which for us are apparently devoid of meaning. These are conflicting harmonics that congest the sound complex, limiting its possibilities, and sometimes distorting the envisaged effect, with a tendency to transform musical sound into noise.

Toleration is greater if the sounds that form a chord belong to melodic lines which underscore the meaning. A sound complex that is difficult to perceive and accept as a chord will appear simple and clear and perfectly tolerable in counterpoint. Musical systems with essentially contrapuntal structures, such as Javanese gamelang music may utilise scales and clashes of melody, which, abstracted as a chord, give much harsher and practically unintelligible formulas. It is very important to consider this element in analysis when studying the scales and structures of Javanese, Cambodian or Thai music. Furthermore, chords may be relatively consonant for certain sound pitches, or with other instruments. This comes from conflicting harmonics, which vary greatly according to the instrument and the various octaves.

In the rhythmic octaves, polyphony gives rise to astonishing sound architecture. Curiously, it is little employed, except in African music and in serious oriental rhythmic music. Good complex polyphony is a fantastic means of expression.

Harmonic or polyphonic structures tend to paralyse the rhythmic due to the duration needed for the harmonic impression to be perceived. It is always necessary to wait a while for the effect of the chord to be digested and perceived. This is, of course, quite contrary to rhythmic vivacity and precision.

Musical Noise and Sounds (Concrete Music)

There is no essential difference between musical noises and sounds, since they are both vibratory complexes. Noise is what we term a complex that is too complicated for us to analyse its components. Indeed, very often, radio sets — for example — transform almost all sounds into noises. Most musical systems utilise noises, owing to their indeterminate melodic character, in order to stress the rhythmic octaves. Musical forms can easily be conceived however, utilising noises and noise ratios so long as they are not perfect noises, have a determined colour and can in fact be broken down into frequency complexes recalling the sound qualities of instruments, but in more complicated forms. One is often astounded, in certain contemporary music, by the lack of research and logic that appears in the form of the noises utilised.

Conclusions

In this brief encounter, it is impossible for us to do more than identify the basic elements needed to establish the morphology of the various musical languages. To penetrate further into the structure of each of these languages, which differ from each other as much as do the great families of spoken languages, would take much more time and work. In order to realise this, it suffices to read a treatise on harmony, an essay on the dodecaphonic theory, Farabi's treatise on musical theory and one of the Sanskrit treatises on intervals and modulated scales. Indeed, almost any study on musical phenomenology and the morphology of the idioms still has to be done. The grammars of the various musical languages have developed in an airtight chamber, each taking for unquestionable assumptions what are often merely incidental and unstable usages.

It is by studying the audio-mental mechanism that links the physical perception of sounds to a mental perception in which the sound becomes an idea, feeling, sensation, that we can begin to lay the bases of logical and intelligible musical systems with immense possibilities, which appear to have been hardly and very erratically explored.

Seen from this standpoint, the study of musical morphology is not merely one of the forms of analysing an art, but it also gives us glimpses of an enthralling science, opening new horizons in the fields of thought, sensation and perception. Through it, we can start to put down in figures our sensorial reactions and even perhaps our ideas; through it, we can start processing the mathematics of thought, find the equations of ideas and feelings. The ancient philosophers had already felt that this was the science of sciences, which would integrate mankind with the cosmos and make the mysterious link between matter and thought. For the Hindus, the Universe is a divine thought, perceived by us as a tangible reality through the illusion of our senses. Music is the key through which we can establish the link that closes the circle formed by thought that creates, matter that transmits and feeling that perceives. But music thus conceived is a science, an art and a technique that is infinitely more ambitious than the sound games we play to amuse ourselves. To understand it, we must take music seriously, be ready to reject the fashions of the day as also the habits of the past and patiently seek the bases of musical language, not in its historical manifestations, but in ourselves, in our physical, physiological and psychic reactions to the different forms taken by sound ratios in the morphology of the various existing or possible musical languages.

~20~

COMPARATIVE MUSICOLOGY :
PRINCIPLES, PROBLEMS, METHODS

A few days ago, Professor Jacques Chailley inaugurated this centre of studies, which would certainly never have been created without his encouragement to its organisers from the very outset, the active interest he has taken in it, and the considerable help he has provided.

With great clarity and congeniality, he has illustrated his reasons for thinking that studying the various systems of oriental music was not only useful in itself, but could also be an important contribution towards a better understanding of the sources of western music.

In speaking to you today on the problems and methods of comparative musicology, I shall in fact often be merely taking up and developing some of the topics that he briefly but clearly put forward the other day.

* * *

There was a time when the world appeared to be wonderfully simple. From Euclid to Darwin, the western mind sought first and foremost unity in science, philosophy and religion. It did its best to create blueprints of an often admirable simplicity, explaining everything, reducing everything to formulas that nowadays may appear somewhat insufficient, attributing to the mind of the creator of the cosmos a mechanism that may even seen simplistic. The laws that govern the universe and ourselves cannot be summarised by a few elementary diagrams. If we manage to formulate rules that seem to apply to a given order of things — which is the object of all science, we must be careful not to apply it to another order of things. Hence the need for a diversity of disciplines that coexist without totally over-lapping. The ancient philosophers and scholars of India as often as not took care not to generalise. They established the principle that what is true according to one mode of experience or particular rea-soning may not be true in another order of ideas. To them, it seemed that reality did not dwell in the unity of things, but in their opposi-tion. It is the antinomies, the incompatibles, that give us the best idea of the nature of things, whence the strange precept in the *Upaniṣads* that the divine is that in which opposites coexist.

We find this law of opposites in all things, and in all disciplines. Our tendency to unite almost inevitably leads to error.

Even in what appears to us as a single formula of experience, music for example, we can never be certain that the various forms of its development are on the same level, are really comparable.

The matter employed by music — sound — is everywhere the same, like its axes, the axis of vibratory frequency and the axis of tempo division. The ways of constructing intelligible structures on these co-ordinates may however vary infinitely. The choice we can make of these structures, to form the different musical languages, depends on our hearing mechanism, the receptivity of our physical ear and the analytical power of our mental organ, which interprets data from the ear and extracts its own emotional and expressive data. Education helps us to develop our perceptions in one sense or an-other and sometimes to attribute a purely conventional meaning to certain relations.

It is the same for spoken language, which, basically, cannot be differentiated from musical language, since it also uses different sound pitches and duration to express feelings or ideas. There are many borderline cases, such as psalmody or chanted recitation in particu-lar, in which what is considered by one culture as a language is inter-preted according to the code of another culture as music. Ethno-musicologists should pay great attention to this case, since the mental process is different and sound means are utilised according to abso-lutely distinct systems of reference. The fact that musical or spoken

160

sounds seem the same does not imply that they have the same meaning, because the system of reference may be wholly different.

I recall a cartoon in which a young American in Paris approached a girl and said "May we?", and she replied "Mais oui" (of course). This perfect harmony owed nothing to the fact that the two protagonists had not perceived that these identical sounds in no way had the same theoretical — or practical — meaning for them both, and that they belonged to two distinct systems of reference. It is frequently the same with musical forms, and we must beware of assimilating what we hear in distant countries as forms similar to the system we are familiar with. This is why, for example, the use of oriental themes in the context of modern dodecaphony, or harmonic chords in the development of oriental modes is, by the very nature of things, as sterile as it is absurd. The problem does not only concern music, but covers all aspects of culture and shows that the colonial effort, the effort to pile one culture on top of another, which may be very well-intentioned, always ends in almost total mental, aesthetic and social confusion.

You may feel that I am straying somewhat from the precise topics that interest us, but I believe it is very important to realise the extent of the problems that arise before establishing practical and useful methods for comparative musicology. Before starting on a long and often wearisome job of notation, measurement and analysis, it is important to be familiar with the basis of the structures we wish to study. I feel that, without that, it might be impossible to make a useful analysis, any more than one can transcribe a language one does not understand.

One of the first elements that plays a highly important role in musical forms is the phenomenon of attention, concentration on a particular aspect, since this has a considerable effect on the musical structure. We may listen to the murmurs of the forest, the song of birds, or street noises in a sort of neutral state of receptivity. As soon as our attention is fixed on the cry of a blackbird or the purring of a scooter, all the other sounds tend to vanish from our consciousness, and are no more than a background noise, which may be more or less pleasant or annoying.

161

This is always the case with music. When we fix our attention on one aspect, we are only relatively conscious of the others. It also acts as a way of escape when, for example, an aspect of the musical scale bothers us: we can then fix our attention on another aspect. Thus the former aspect no longer bothers us, because it is no longer in the area floodlit by our mental projector. This may lead us to an initial classification of musical forms. We shall see that, in musical systems in which the scale structure is very precise, or the exactitude of the interval plays a major role, the rhythmic aspect is of secondary importance. Indeed, in some long melodic expositions, the rhythmic aspect is absent or imprecise: there is phrasing, metre, as in spoken language, but no constant independent rhythm. On the other hand, when attention is fixed first and foremost on the rhythm, we are relatively indifferent to melodic exactitude, a wrong note passes unnoticed, whereas the slightest slip in the rhythm makes the concert hall wild. We have a very good example of this in true jazz.

When the melodic scale and the rhythmic scale are weak, which often happens for technical reasons, musical expression takes refuge in other aspects and our attention gets fixed on something else. This is why the relations of sound colour and volume play such an important part in western music. In piano music in particular, the melodic scale is neutral and imprecise, varying quite considerably according to tuner and tonality. The rhythmic scale is extremely weak, as in all written music, boiling down to an irregular beat and a tempo division that is in fact more metric than rhythmic, as conceived by the Blacks or Orientals. Sound volume ratios reach incredible subtlety however, the touch becomes the most extraordinary means of expression, and subtle differences of spacing lend a great pianist means of expression — which we are moreover incapable of hearing — which are not at all inferior to those of other systems.

In vocal and orchestral music, the colour of sound, timbre comes into play. It is all the same to us that the brass, woodwind, harps and strings follow scales that are only relatively equivalent. We do not listen to that, but to their timbre, their colour. The same happens with a forte vibrato voice, which has very little in common with the precise voices of singers of modal music. When someone tells me, "What I don't like in Indian music are those nasal voices, without relief", if I wish to be polite, which happens on occasion, I avoid saying "It's because you don't listen to the music". Indians are just the same, and I have often heard, "I love Beethoven's symphonies, it's only the noise of the orchestra that bothers me. Do they never play them without accompaniment?".

You can see that comparative music is not something easy. That is the precise reason why it can become such a great enrichment, since it forces us to penetrate different forms of musical thought and feeling. In return, this will help us to understand better what, in the evolution of our own music, is either logical and consistent, or else arbitrary and without a future.

But since we are all specialists here, I think you will expect me to say a few words on the technical work and study methods that, despite everything, may help us to compare musical systems. We must, of course, study each form of music, each musical system, in all its aspects — whether they are strong or weak. I believe it is essential to decide first of all what is the dominant aspect, because this is the one that will give us the key to the whole system, the other aspects playing merely a somewhat ornamental role.

We must first find out whether the dominant is modal or melodic (two very different things), whether it is rhythmic or only metrical, whether timbres are important or volume ratios, or anything else at all. Once the dominant has been established, we must analyse its characteristics very carefully, because it is there that we shall find the precision that gives value to the system. We shall then see — when we analyse them in turn — that the other aspects tend to be the more imprecise the stronger the dominant.

This is how to proceed:

Recording Methods

Choice and moment
Control
Verification

Scale Analysis

Vocal scales and instrumental scales
Problem of the tonic
Melodic scales and modal scales
Tetrachord and octave
Polyphony and modal counterpoint
Ornaments

Rhythmic Analysis

Beat
The rhythmic context: strong and weak tempos
Rhythmic variations in the context
Atīta and *anāgata* countertime
Change of rhythm and acceleration

Recitation, Psalmody and Melody

Rhythmical framework and metric framework

Notation and Improvisation

Need to Standardise Methods

~21~

CATEGORIES OF INTERVALS OR ŚRUTI-JĀTIS

There are two main approaches in interpreting ancient texts on music. Some believe that the ancient musicians may have had peculiar tastes and enjoyed intervals and musical forms which to us appear as unpleasant dissonances. Others consider that the fundamental laws of consonance, being physical laws, must be true for all men at all times, and consequently allege that there is no reason to suppose that these laws were not valid for ancient Indian music. The fact that a few mediaeval works provide confused or inaccurate definitions of the intervals may not necessarily mean that the music and musicians were wrong, but only that the theoreticians had insufficient means for analysing and recording the intervals. This should not surprise us, since most modern books on Indian music give for *Śrutis* lists of vibration-numbers, all of which are grossly mistaken, as can easily be shown with the help of accurate instruments for measuring intervals. An example of how books can be misleading can be seen from the following event. In the 19th century, a German physicist made a mistake in his learned calculations on the resonance of horns. The figures he used implied that an E flat horn would need to be 18.77 meters (over 56 feet) long. This glaring mistake has however since been reproduced in technical treatises on instruments in several European languages, since nobody has ever taken the trouble to verify the calculations. We can easily imagine future scholars devising wonderful theories about this giant trumpet and the people who blew it, just as they make superior assertions about the strange scales that pleased the ear of ancient musicians.

Unless there is definite proof to the contrary, we should never take it for granted that ancient musicians ever went astray from the fundamental consonances, which are by far the easiest intervals to play and recognise accurately. On the other hand, we can easily understand that difficulties in analysing or measuring intervals may lead to slightly inaccurate definitions.

Before attempting to interpret the ancient authors, we should do them the courtesy of making sure that we ourselves have sufficient knowledge of the physical possibilities of sound, which they may have been at pains to describe. We may then suddenly discover that what seemed at first to be an arbitrary classification turns out to be merely a slightly odd way of expressing some fundamental law of physics.

The *Śruti-jātis* or categories of intervals, classified according to the kind of expression they convey, are given with some variation in different Sanskrit works on music. These have given rise to various interpretations, often accompanied by alleged frequencies which, fortunately, convey nothing to the reader, nor usually, I believe, to the writer either.

It may therefore be of interest to see whether any classification similar to that of the *Śruti-jātis* can be obtained from a physical study of intervals.

According to the Bharata method for tuning the Vīṇā, there is very little doubt that the old *Pramāṇa śruti* was the interval we now call the comma. If we tune the different notes of the scale by successive fifths (*pañcama-saṁvādī* = 3/2), which is the most consonant and easiest of all intervals to tune, we obtain, after the third fifth, intervals which seem to be high. To obtain intervals more consonant with the starting note, we have to lower by one comma (81/80) the intervals obtained by fifths. This is one of the basic problems of music, which we find expressed and solved in different ways in the musical theory of all countries. The *Nāṭya Śāstra* is not sufficiently explicit to allow us to say for certain that the *Ṣaḍja* and *Madhyama grāma* should thus correspond to what we now know as the Pythagorean and Harmonic scales with the typical difference of one comma in most of their intervals, corresponding to a Cosmic, Solar-Lunar, active-passive character on the one hand, and an emotional, Mars-Venus, desire-enjoyment character on the other. It is however very probable that the differentiation of the *Grāmas* must originally have been of that order, since this is the only kind of really fundamental difference that fully justifies classification according to *Grāmas*.

The First Śruti-Jāti

If we follow the simplest mode of tuning by ascending fifths, we obtain a series of intervals which all have a similar expression. The first five intervals of this series, beginning from *Sā*, are (1) *Pañcama* ($3^2/2^3$), (2) *Ṛṣabha* (9/8 or 3/2), (3) the high *Dhaivata*[1], which we may term *Dha* + (27/16 or $3^3/2^4$), (4) the high *Gandhāra* or *Ga*+ (81/64 or $3^4/2^6$), (5) *Ni* + (243/128 or $3^5/2^7$). Further intervals are not used in music because they come to be almost identical with simple intervals, as we shall presently see.

All these intervals have a common character. They all express sunshine, joy, activity, but on a rather abstract plane. They form what we may term, in the Chinese way, the Solar aspect of the cosmic series. We can see that, from the point of view of number, they all correspond to ratios formed exclusively by the successive powers of 3 divided by the corresponding powers of 2. This is the first *Śruti-Jāti* or class of interval.

The Second Śruti-Jāti

If we start again from the original *Sā* and proceed by descending fifths (or ascending fourths), we obtain the five intervals: (1) *Madhyama* (4/3 or $2^2/3$); (2) the common *Komala Niṣāda* — which we may term natural *Komala Niṣāda* or *Nī kn* (16/9 or $2^4/3^2$); (3) *Gā kn* (32/27 or $2^5/3^4$); (4) *Dhā kn* (128/81 or $2^7/3^5$); and (5) the low *Komala Ṛṣabha* or *Ṛk* - 256/243 or $2^8/3^6$).

---

[1] The notes of the more usual diatonic scale will be marked *n* (natural), or be without any sign. Notes raised by one, two and three commas will be marked +, ++, +++. Notes lowered by one, two, and three commas will be marked -, - -, - - -.

The common character of all these intervals is one of moonlight, peace, passivity. They form the lunar aspect of the basic or cosmic series. They all have as denominator the successive powers of 3, with the corresponding power of 2 as numerator.

The Third Śruti-Jāti

The intervals of the double (ascending and descending) series of fifths are, as we have seen, rather abstract in expression; and the ascending ones are often high in pitch. If we bring the high *Dha* – (27/16) down to the more consonant and softer harmonic *Dha* (5/3) and then proceed by fifths as before, taking this *Dha* as our new basis, we obtain a series of intervals which all are one comma (81/80) below those of the basic series. The ascending fifths of this new series are rarely used in music because of their exaggeratedly weak character. They are the *Re*– (10/9 or 5 x 2/3): *Pa*– (40/27 or 5 x 2/3): *Sā*– (160/81 or 5 x 2/3) and *Ma*– (320/243 or 5 x 2/3): *Sā*– (160/81 or 5 x 2/3) and *Ma*– 320/243 or 5 x 2/3).

The descending series on the other hand contains some of the main intervals in music, which are, beside the basic *Dha* 5/3, (1) *Ga* (5/4 or 5/2): (2) n *Ni* (15/8 or 5 x 3/2): (3) the low *Tīvra Madhyama*, *Ma–T* (45/32 or 5x3/2) and (4) *Re k*– 135/128 or 5 x 3/2).

All these intervals have a common character of soft emotion, enjoyment, satisfaction, which is the feeling of the qualities shown by the second or descending series.

We see that the last interval here is called *Re k*… like the 5th one in the basic descending series. In fact, these two intervals are practically identical, their difference being only of 0.49 *savarts* (1.96 cents) i.e. about 1/10th of a comma, or 1/50th of a tone. Any further fifth would in practice coincide with those of the other series. The development of fifths in this type of scale is therefore by its very nature limited to five.

We may note that all the intervals of this series have in common the number 5 as numerator, multiplied by powers of 3/2.

168

The Fourth Śruti-Jāti

By a similar process, if we raise the intervals of the basic series by one comma, we obtain a series which has 5 as its denominator, multiplied by the powers of 2/3. These intervals will express passion, desire, etc., i.e. the qualities shown by the first series.

We obtain first, as the basic note, the high *Ga k* + (6/5 or 2 x 3/5). Of the ascending fifths (*Ni k* + 9/5, *Ma* + 27/20, *Sā* + 81/80, *Pa* + 243/160), only the first one is normally used in music, the others being harsh and brutal. The descending series on the other hand has beautiful passionate intervals 1) *Dha k* + (8/5 or 2/5): *Re Kn* (16/15 or 2/5 x 3); 3 *Ma Tn* (64/45 or 2/5 x 3): (4) *Ni* + (256/125 or 2/5 x 3).

The Fifth Śruti-Jāti

A series that lies two commas above the basic series is extremely harsh and is hardly used in music. The series two commas below the basic series has, on the other hand, five intervals expressing intense sadness and distress, which are used in the most moving *rāgas*.

The basic note of this series is *Ma T-*(25/18 or 5/3 x 2), followed by *Ri k-*925/24 or 5/3 x 2); *Dha k-*(25/16 or 5/2), *Ga k-*(75/64 or 5 x 3/2) and *Ni k-*(225/128 or 5x3/2).

The Circle of Śrutis

As we have seen, the fifth note of each series melts into the next series. If we now take two other series, the - - - or + + +, we find that they are both practically identical. This completes the cycle of the possible intervals in the comma scale, giving a total of fifty-three possible *Śrutis* (which become the old 66, if we introduce at each half tone the intermediate sounds called quartertones). The last series, as well as the + + series, are not normally used in music. We therefore have five groups of intervals with different types of ratios, corresponding to different categories of expression, as can easily be ascertained on any instrument for measuring intervals. This classification includes

all the simple intervals used in music. It seems beyond any doubt that
the theories of *Śruti-Jātis* or categories of intervals — *Madhya, Āyata,
Mṛdu, Dīpta* and *Karuṇā* — must have been based on this physical
fact and correspond respectively to the above series. The dropping of
some intervals less frequently used, as well as some confusion in the
works of mediaeval writers who may not have been thoroughly con-
versant with the arithmetic of sound, should not deter us from bear-
ing in mind that the *Śruti-Jātis* were first and foremost a physical
fact, before becoming a theory of Sanskrit writers on music.

~22~

ELEMENTS IN THE FORMATION
OF SCALES BEYOND RESONANCE

EXPRESSIVE DEFORMATIONS

When I received the preliminary plan for this symposium, I was surprised by the slightly pejorative terms used to define the subject on which I was asked to speak. I fear I may feel a little like the defendant in a concert of virtuous homage to harmonics, suspected of abducting minor intervals. The term "expressive deformations" makes one think of ancient grievances against musicians who insist on pulling on the strings to produce the different sounds for the right pitch. It appears that this problem has changed very little since Antiquity.

Whoever has attempted to understand the strange phenomenon of musical intervals — which means all of us — has sought an arithmetical formula to justify the place and number of intervals used by musicians. Many highly ingenious systems have been invented to establish the scale of intervals, using very different methods. Thus, it has been possible to establish scales that are apparently very close to one another, although often profoundly different in principle and substance, from the cycle of fifths to tempered fourths. However, we find that theoreticians are always annoyed by the fact that musicians, and the best in particular, do not appear to comply exactly with the intervals of any system. They always stray from it a little whenever they have the chance to do so, and it is this very deviation that seems to be one of the sources of musical expression. This leads us directly to the question that I must ask you, as I have asked myself, What are these expressive deformations? Are they really deformations, or on the contrary, are they fundamental elements of musical vocabulary? Could it not be that the theoretical systems proposed are too simplistic or too abstract, tending to systematise too much on insufficient data? I believe that the problems we are dealing with come essentially from systematic deformations based on theoretical conceptions that are too elementary, instead of starting from a properly scientific observation of musical facts. However, we no longer live in an age of cosmological speculation and our approach to musical phenomena may sometimes appear, from the point of view of other disciplines, almost prehistoric.

The first fact to attract our attention is that most systems for analysing the scale have been established since the ancient Greeks, and are based on observation of the acoustic properties of musical instruments and the practical methods used to tune them. It is quite clear that vocal melody existed long before the use of melodic instruments, and this is still the case of some peoples who possess extremely developed musical systems. Furthermore, it appears that our melodic thought inevitably maintains this dependence on the voice, since the voice is in some way the organ of action of the auditive system. Even today, composers who do not work exclusively on abstract compositions tend to hum or whistle the succession of intervals or the melodic form that comes to their mind, before transcribing it in a scale of instrumental intervals that seems to them approximately the same as the one they are expressing vocally. Even at this point, they must distort their thought in order to transcribe it in a limited notation system, corresponding to the predetermined tunings of certain instruments.

The question that arises is whether the intervals, which seem to play a dominant role in the resonance of instruments and in practical tuning methods, are as important in purely vocal or mental melody. I feel that the answer should be emphatically: No. A perfect fifth is in no way a more important melodic interval than a major second or a minor third, and the fact that the second is a fifth of a fifth does not have any reflection on the melodic and expressive character that is

172

proper to the second. There is nothing in the expression of the second sung in a tune that makes us realise immediately its dependence on the fifth, despite a certain relationship that makes them classifiable in the same family of intervals that we may call strong, active, major, virile. Melodically, the second is much more important than the fifth, and most of the world's psalmodies and even some highly developed melodic forms are based on the second and only accidentally reach the fifth.

Should we then consider that resonance, that phenomenon of harmonics, plays no role in musical structure? Absolutely not! It may be, however, a secondary phenomenon, a strange property of sounding bodies, as useful as the beat for the tuning of instruments, but does not suffice, without the intervention of other acoustic properties, to justify scale structure and melodic expression.

Given the current fashion for non-Euclidean geometries, I find it better to leave to one side an old observation in physics which only allows the fourth to appear as the behaviour of an interval, invoking the ear's tolerance starting from the fifth note and explaining nothing of the complexity of expressive, i.e. properly musical, intervals. It is not without interest to note that, even in contemporary western music, modulation, which largely depends on the relationship of the fifths and the harmonies that inspire resonance, has made considerable progress ever since the fifth was broken, tempered, strained, i.e. when we passed into the sphere of tempered dodecaphonism. The latter has nothing to do with resonance and requires a theory of ear tolerance that clearly allows us to invent any sound system we wish containing sounds close enough to the ones our melodic instinct leads us to employ, but which explain nothing about its nature.

Whichever musical system we seek to analyse, we find that all the scales utilise a limited number of intervals, located in certain regions of the octave. It remains for us to analyse what these intervals are, how many they are, their relative importance and emotional meaning, the expressive value attributed to them. The harmonic scale only gives us four usable sounds. The cycle of fifths gives us five, which are not the same ones. Such sounds, if they are usable, are not a majority and are far from the intervals used melodically. We must seek elsewhere for the source of expressive intervals. It is only by taking into account real musical elements that are much easier to analyse today than in the past, that we can establish certain laws explaining the phenomenon of concordance and of expression, taking into account both the physiological phenomenon of hearing and the psychological phenomenon of expression.

We may leave temperament aside as a brutal method, invented by instrument manufacturers for convenience's sake. Whether we divide the octave into seven equal tones, twelve semi-tones, 22, 36 or 52, we come rather closer to expressive vocal intervals, but we are forever establishing neutral scales in which there is nothing that can logically justify the particular role or expressive character of certain intervals. One day, M. Ansermet explained to me that he thought that we have a logarithmic mind and are sensitive to multiples of the twelfth roots of two. This would imply a mental mechanism that a performing circus horse might dream of, but all the same does not explain why we prefer twelfth roots rather than thirteenth or eleventh and would also imply that the fifth and harmonic third would appear out of tune, which seems not to be the case.

In musical systems where great importance is given to the precision of what are considered to be expressive intervals, a division of the octave is consciously or unconsciously reached providing 28 tones, the minimum being 22. Within these divisions, the intervals seem to be grouped together in families, as in Hindu theory. These groupings are encountered in one form or other in all theories, since we also speak of a minor third or seventh and a major third and seventh, thereby implying an expressive, even though rudimentary, relationship.

As far as expression is concerned, we may note a double structure in the acoustic scales. A preliminary overall division allows us to say that this is a sixth, or a third. An expressive subdivision then leads us to say that this D sharp is somewhat higher, but above all more brilliant, more joyful, more intense than the E flat, indicating expressive nuances that we were previously unable to note, but which can

174

now be done with great precision using magnetic tape and measuring instruments, if we take the trouble.

We shall observe that, in the sound scale, certain notes have several variations, all of which seem in tune, but with distinct expressions, whereas other notes seem fixed, and in their case any deviation appears to be displeasing and purposeless. In my opinion, the best reference system we possess is the Indian one, because it is by far the most complete. It goes without saying that its positive data apply totally to the intervals of Iranian and Arab music and to the various kinds of popular music, as well as to western vocal music, as soon as it can escape instrumental tyranny and abandon itself to emotional impropriety.

The fixed notes of the scale in modal form, starting from a given tonic, are (with the tonic) the second and fifth, of which I have never remarked any expressive variations. The fourth is usually fixed, but I have had the chance to note — and also to play — a fourth lowered by one comma which, employed with caution, gives an extraordinarily melancholy colour to an apparently major mode such as the Indian *Bilāval* mode.

The major third, the major sixth and the major seventh have two positions, one corresponding to the intervals of the cycle of fifths, which we may call Pythagorean, giving glorious, vibrant, aggressive expressions, and those that are sometimes called harmonic, evoking an idea of sweetness, charm, and tranquillity.

The widest variety appears in the intermediate intervals. In Indian music — and indeed in all music — there are three kinds of minor thirds and minor sixths and four kinds of minor seconds, minor sevenths, or augmented fourths. The minor notes, which have only three variants, are those in which the simplest harmonic relation is sharp. In each case, therefore, there is an apparently simple harmonic relation, corresponding to the most usual expression of the interval, and two lower expressive variants. Only in three cases do we have a higher expressive variant with a very different character.

If we start from purely experimental data based on measurements made when the musician plays with feeling — since it goes without saying that the expressive interval only appears with the expression — we always find the same intervals, which seem to correspond to relatively simple long-known proportional ratios. These are the minor semi-tone, the limma and the major semi-tone, which can hardly be considered novelties. We must not exclude the possibility of other very close ratio formulas, which would help to explain better their psycho-auditive reactions that appear to be almost universal. Using proper instruments on which these intervals can be played easily, their character is immediately evident.

Each of these groups of minor sounds presents parallels, differences and relationships with other groups. The various minor seconds are related to the minor sixths and the minor thirds to the minor sevenths. It is somewhat difficult to enter into the details of these expressive nuances without a proper demonstration. On the whole, however, for the intervals we may call minor, in each case — leaving aside the augmented fourths — we find a peaceful, tender, luminous interval, followed at about one comma lower down, by an erotic, amorous and intense interval, followed still lower by a melancholic, hopeless, desolating interval.

Owing to a curious phenomenon, augmented fourth intervals appear to function in reverse order. Although the isolated sounds are not very expressive, they have the capacity to intensify the expression of other intervals.

Using the frequency ratios that appear to correspond to these expressive intervals, we can make certain observations about their numerical characteristics. I believe that these, if we co-ordinate our observations with the right instruments, would easily allow us to formulate a theory on musical scales based on our psychological reactions and our auditive and mental ability to analyse the ratios, rather than basing ourselves on the peculiarities of string resonance and sound bodies.

The observation of what appear to be the limits of our audio-mental power to perceive and analyse intervals, both physically as pleasant and recognisable concordances or discords, and mentally as expressions, has led me to establish a scale of expressive intervals made of combined cycles. These include the cycle of fourths, the cycles of major and minor thirds, never going in any way beyond the fifth multiplicatory factor, which seems to be a kind of limit to our power of mental analysis, with the result that any more complex frequency ratio appears unpleasant and meaningless to us. This limit may vary slightly according to the individual. Thus established, the families of numerical ratios seem to match the families of expressive intervals. Such a system naturally includes the first harmonics and the first fifths of the cycle of fifths, but seeks to reduce the problems of musical scales to the psycho-physiological phenomenon of perceiving expressive sound ratios, instead of attempting to find a solution in the physical resonance of objects or in purely mathematical successions.

I have myself worked only on highly developed musical systems, or on popular forms coexisting with developed systems. I believe that it would be very interesting to make similar observations on really isolated systems of primitive music, in each case seeking to determine, as the basic element for the formation of musical scales, the human ear's limits of discrimination and the attributions of definite expressions to the various intervals.

Report of the Discussion

Mr. Chailley asked Mr. Daniélou whether, in classifying the intervals into various categories of expression, he considered them all as being on the same level, or whether he thought that in some cases, but not in others, there is some additional expressive factor.

Mr. Daniélou replied that, in his own experience, the intervals themselves, even when mechanically reproduced, had an impact or expression. It is not due to any intent or feeling on the part of the musician.

For Mr. Chailley, certain feelings are translated by the deformation of certain intervals, which, without the feelings themselves, would be different. This fact is borne out in a great number of cases, as for example, if the violinist or singer trained on the tempered system mechanically repeats what he has learnt, he will give tempered intervals. This is not the case if he attempts to put some expressive content into his playing, when he will be led to leave the limitations of temperament owing to the need to strengthen or augment certain intervals, by augmenting the expressive differences of these intervals to the extent that he wishes to intensify the dynamic feeling. It has often been observed that players of string instruments — violinists, cellists, etc. — or singers tend to come close, not to the tempered scale, but to the Pythagorean scale, which gives more dynamism to certain intervals, making what is major "more major", what is minor "more minor", what is stringendo "more stringendo". … The harmonic solution has the contrary effect, which is to smooth out differences, raise what is stringendo, lower what is high, so there is a conflict between the two solutions.

About twenty years ago, "Monde Musical" held a discussion between two famous cellists, Diran Alexanian and Paul Bazelaire. The former championed "expressive music", and the latter "mathematical or absolute precision". They represented two different western schools of hearing, one restricting itself to the learnt model, and the other deforming and reinforcing it for the purpose of expression. Our ear is already deformed from the start by a tempered education, a purely arbitrary operation. Eastern musicians are untouched by this initial deformation.

Mr. Tran Van Khé stated that, in Vietnamese music, under neutral conditions, a melodic pattern is not performed with any given intention, but that certain intervals have the property of intensifying expression. Singers enjoy a great deal of freedom in their means of expression. Only strong measures have to be kept to, while improvisation can be used with weak measures. There are some nuances that express serenity, sadness, and a modal system expressing joy. The fourth approximates to the perfect fourth, the augmented fourth has the property of intensifying expression and accentuating the expression of sad intervals. The minor seventh is considered to be a sad interval. Mr. Tran Van Khé then sang three specimens illustrating a modification of embellishment and a slight interval variation.

Following the details given by Mr. Tran Van Khé, Mr. Chailley came to the following conclusion: the impression of sadness (meaning feelings added to the neutral expression of non-corrected music) is exercised for expressive ends. In other words, starting from an initial non-corrected input, it is corrected for expressive purposes — assuming the pre-existence or non-existence of this initial input. When an oriental musician does this for expressive purposes, is it by absolute qualification of the interval without any term of comparison, or is it by comparison with a typical interval which itself expresses this feeling?

For Mr. Daniélou, it is a matter of the different intervals, which he classifies in groups as a matter of convenience. What is important is the real interval and the expression it represents. In Iranian music, there are slightly raised minor intervals called *Khoron*. Such intervals, which are also found in Indian music, are defined by their expression. In order to sing a sad minor third, the singer gives an interval that is technically a perfect interval, which the musician can reach more easily through feeling that through other means. Speaking of neutral intervals, what is usually meant are intervals that are not in tune, sung by people who will sing almost anything, because they have not entered the feeling.

Mr. Chailley finally came to the capital question for European music. Where do the feelings of sadness attributed to the minor and of gaiety attributed to the major come from? At first glance, the major appears gay because it is wider — and therefore has a greater extension — but in Vietnamese music, the perfect fourth appears neutral, without any expression, or with a serene if not gay expression, whereas the augmented fourth seems sad, thus contrary to what westerners believe: extending upwards gives an impression of sadness.

In seeking common ground between the two explanations, Mr. Chailley suggests that the impression of gaiety and relaxation generally leads to regular intervals given by the expected mode of formation (i.e. intervals of the cycle of fifths utilising as a unit of measurement the fifth or fourth provided by the resonance). In both cases and in the two used by Mr. Daniélou, the intervals theoretically given by the cycle of fifths or related processes are replaced by a deformation of the interval generating the impression of sadness. As far as the minor third is concerned, we are no longer in the context of a chord of resonance — the major chord is itself the chord of resonance, i.e. the transcription of the harmonics 1-6 — since, in resonance, the minor chord is a deformation of the third. There are also other similar examples of the deformation of intervals, such as the sad intervals mentioned by Mr. Tran Van Khé.

Mr. Daniélou remarked that different terminologies were being used in the discussion. In speaking of the minor third, what should really be compared are the different kinds of minor third: i.e. the minor third 6 : 5 is a minor third that is considered rather gay. Mr. Chailley noted that his colleague was speaking of melodic intervals, whereas he was speaking of harmonic intervals. This would lead to a very different point of view, because in melodic intervals, the minor third is not an artificial interval, but belongs both to the cycle of fifths and to pure resonance. What is artificial is to give it, harmonically, the role that resonance attributes to the major third.

Mr. Daniélou specified that harmony can use different thirds that are more or less concordant. The major chord has no "expressive" ratio. Together with the Pythagorean third, this chord sounds like a trumpet, whereas the truly harmonic third is sweet and tranquil.

Mr. Chailley recognised the truth of this, because, starting from a western scheme, based on an ear which has assimilated the set of harmonics from 1 to 6, the neutral scheme is the resonance, the low third, the harmonic fifth. Raising it to the Pythagorean third, a supplementary tonus is added that is not in the scheme. In the case of the minor third, a greater deformation is made in the opposite sense. The initial scheme is instinctive and not reasoned: the musician's ear instinctively and harmonically hears the chord of resonance, i.e. the neutral chord of the low third which he is under the impression of toning up if he raises his third, and, contrariwise, of restricting if he lowers it to the minor. In the case of the melodic third, this phenomenon does not apply. The simple harmonic has nothing to do with it, because the starting point is not a harmonic chord of three notes. Mr. Daniélou's objection is thus precisely as Mr. Chailley has suggested, i.e. in the classical melodic scheme, the construction of deformation used as an example comes from the cycle of fifths. It is precisely in this case that the minor third — unlike the harmonic scheme — is the starting point: the schemes are rigorously inverted.

In considering "unaccompanied melody", i.e. "cycle of fifths", priority is given to the minor third.

In considering "western harmony", from the 16th century onwards, the starting point is the chord of resonance, i.e. the major third, and the psychological components are rigorously inverted as far as the third is concerned. On the one hand we have the predominance of the minor third, and on the other the predominance of the major third.

Mr. Daniélou added that there is no system of modal music in which the complement of the interval is considered as the interval and that, in playing a tonic, C for example, then the lower G, one hears a fifth and not a fourth. The expression of the G remains that of a fifth, and has nothing to do with that of a fourth. Theoretically, it is a fourth, whereas musically, it is not.

To Mr. Chailley, who asked him whether he was speaking melodically or harmonically, M. Daniélou replied that from the point of view of expression, in speaking of the fundamentals of a chord, one would come more or less to the same conclusions. From a melodic and modal point of view, the principles also apply in the case of chords, even for a note considered as fundamental and tonic.

Mr. Daniélou agreed with Mr. Chailley that the initial scheme is entirely different, but believed that the expression obtained by the two systems reaches "expressive similarities". The natural possibilities of utilising intervals in chords are much less, and consequently intervals are much less considered. In each case the same level is reached: it is not by chance that — both melodically and harmonically — the Pythagorean third is deemed strong and glorious, and the harmonic third is melodically sweet and peaceful.

Mr. Chailley deemed that these facts support his theory, i.e. the occurrence of a deformation starting from the initial scheme, as the element of expression.

~23~

MANTRA
PRINCIPLES OF LANGUAGE AND MUSIC
ACCORDING TO HINDU COSMOLOGY

Hindu cosmology poses the fundamental problem of the possibility of communication, the principle on which the different forms of language are based: the languages of smell, taste, touch, the visual languages of gesture and symbols, the language of sound with its two branches of spoken and musical language. Hindu philosophers consider that the Universe, starting from an initial manifestation of energy, develops according to the principles contained in its germ, according to a kind of genetic code based on mathematical data.

Originally formed by purely energetic ratios, the world develops its multiple forms, utilising the same basic formulas. Every manifestation of matter, life, perception, or sensation, are parallel branches coming from a common tree.

It is the basic identity of the energy components of matter, life, thought and perception that allow us to establish relations, analogies, between one and another. In this way, a visual or sound language can help us to evoke certain aspects of thought, feeling, emotion, and the harmony of forms. If there were no relationship, one language could not serve as a vehicle for the other.

In the logic of creation, a world only exists if it is perceived. There is no perception without an object, no object without perception. Each state of matter corresponds to a perceptive sense and a form of consciousness among living beings. In places perpetually without light, fish have no eyes. Our auditory perceptions, particularly in music, are extremely important, because they are what we can most easily analyse in terms of frequency ratios, in numerical terms. Through the phenomenon of language, whether musical or articulated, we can discover something about these equations that are the basis for the structures of matter, life, perception and thought. This is why the ancients always considered music as a sort of key to all sciences.

It is consequently not idiotic to seek, as did the philosophers of the ancient world, parallels and affinities between the details that reveal musical intervals and different forms of matter and life, plants, animals, the structures of atoms or of the planetary systems, as well as the mechanisms of perception, emotional reactions or the structures of thought. To understand them, it is sufficient to put them in equation form, to work them out.

In a general fashion, we may call language the body of processes utilised by living beings as a means of expression or communication. A language is formed by a set of symbols that represent and evoke objects, persons, actions, emotions, feelings, and even abstract principles. Like all symbolic systems, however, language can never be more than an approximation, or evocation. It can only indicate, suggest an idea, form, person, feeling, emotion, and can never really represent them.

Any means of communication is by definition a language. Different kinds of language are classified in a hierarchy that reflects the states of matter or elements and the perceptive senses to which they correspond.

The element of fire, the sphere of sight, corresponds to the visual forms of language. To this domain belong the *yantras*, or symbolic diagrams, as well as images, hieroglyphs and, to a certain extent, writing, as visual forms of communication. Also linked to the sphere of sight is the language of gesture, or *mudrās*, which can be a very complete means of communication. Ritual actions, allowing communication with the invisible world of the spirits, are largely tied to the language of *mudrās*.

The basic element is called ether. It is the domain in which the other elements can develop. The characteristics of this element are

183

space and time. A wave is characterised by its length and frequency. Its perception is thus linked to the relative value of our perception of space and time. Beings living in other dimensions, with a different perception of time, are unknowable to us. Our efforts to communicate with subtle beings, spirits, assume that they perceive the same time duration as we do. This is why such efforts are often sterile. A god, for whom a day may correspond to a human lifetime, is not on the same wavelength as we are, and communication is difficult.

In its origin, all that exists is merely the manifestation of energy of a vibratory nature in space-time, which is ether. We have no organ that can perceive ether vibrations directly. If we had, we would know the secret nature of the world, and its formation process. We only perceive simple vibrations through their repercussions on the air. This is the domain of sound. As the closest representation to the process through which the Creator's thought is manifest in the universe, sound appears to be the most suitable tool for expressing, albeit in a limited manner, the different aspects of the world, of being and of thought.

There are two kinds of sound language. If we use only the numerical ratios between sound vibrations — similar to the geometric ratios of the *yantra* — we obtain musical language. When we utilise the peculiarities of our vocal organ to interrupt, differentiate and rhythm the sounds, we obtain spoken language, which allows us to fashion a large variety of distinct sound symbols that can be utilised to represent objects, notions, and circumscribe, roughly, the forms of thought. This is the domain of the *mantras*.

The world is insubstantial. It is a divine dream, an illusion to which divine power lends an appearance of reality. The world is only pure energy, tensions, vibrations, whose simplest expression appears in the phenomenon of sound. This is why it is said that the Creator utters the Universe. It is the theory of the Divine Word. The world is only a word, a divine song through which the Creator's ideation is expressed. This is why, when, through the introspection of *yoga*, we go back to the point at which thought becomes word, where emotion is born from musical sound, we manage to understand something of the way in which the divine being gives birth to the world and to life.

184

During this introspection, we may observe that thought is manifested in language in four stages. It first appears in an unformed substrate called *parā*, the beyond, then wells forth as a precise and indivisible entity, of which we suddenly have a kind of global vision. This stage is called *paśyantī*, the vision. We then seek to circumscribe its contours with the aid of sound symbols, or words. This formulation is more or less precise according to the richness of the available vocabulary, the number and quality of the words that we have learned to utilise. This stage of the mental formulation of the idea through words is called *madhyamā*, the intermediate stage. We may then exteriorise this formulation in a sound form known as *vaikharī*, speech. It can also be expressed however by gestures, or *mudrās*.

Going back to the sources of speech is one of the major techniques of *yoga*. The process of manifesting the idea by sound takes place through the body's subtle centres, or *cakras*, speech helping us to perceive the reality. Following the path of speech manifestation backwards, starting from the *vaikharī* form in the centre of the throat, we can reach the formulation stage, *madhyamā*, in the *cakra* located in the region of the heart. We can then obtain the vision, *paśyantī*, ideation, the apparition of the idea, in the bulbous centre located at the height of the navel. Finally, beyond the idea, we can reach the substrate of thought, blending in the *mūlādhāra*, the centre of energy coiled up at the base of the spine. This return to the source of language is one of the most effective methods of attaining a perception of the unformed beatitude of the divine. *Mantra-yoga*, which uses articulated sound, and *svara-yoga*, which goes back to the source of musical sound, are essential aspects of the spiritual experience that is the ultimate goal of *yoga*.

It is only starting from the *madhyamā* stage, formulation, that we can analyse the relationship between thought and language. We then discover that the potential of language is extremely restricted. The limitations of our perceptions, of our ear's power to discriminate, mean that we can effectively distinguish and utilise only fifty-four articulated sounds, which we call vowels and consonants. These form the material with which all articulated sound formulas are constructed, all *mantras*, as well as all the words used in every language. It is with this reduced amount of material that we must construct nouns, verbs and adjectives that allow us to determine, more or less adequately, the contours of an idea. A veritable inner conflict now takes place, as we seek the words that will allow us to express the idea, although we never do more than determine its approximate outline. Sound elements are like tokens that we line up to draw the contours of our thought. That is why it is dangerous — and sometimes absurd — to mistake words for ideas.

In music, we shall encounter a similar problem, since we can only discern fifty-four distinct sounds in the octave, which the Hindus call *śruti*, "that which can be heard". This figure of fifty-four appears to indicate the limit of our possibility of perception and mental classification. As with all the senses, these limitations determine our vision of the world, what we are destined to perceive and consequently our role in Creation. We have parallel limitations in our perception of colours, forms, tastes, odours. The set of articulated and musical elements forming the totality of sound material available to us thus numbers one hundred and eight. This is one of the reasons for which this number is itself deemed sacred, representing for mankind the totality of the Word. In the gestation of the world, in the formulation of divine thought, this figure corresponds to certain numerical codes that we shall find in all aspects of creation.

It is relatively easy to explain the limitations of our musical perceptions, since sound ratios can be analysed and expressed in terms of numerical ratios. This mathematical aspect also allows us to establish the relationships between musical sounds and the *yantras* — or geometrical symbols, as well as with harmonies, the proportions that determine what appears to us as beauty. The sacred sculptures of India are based on very strict proportional canons. A god's image is thus a figurative form based on a *yantra* and has proportional characteristics similar to those that unite the notes of a *rāga* — a musical mode — or the elements of a *mantra*, which is the corresponding articulated form.

A cosmic principle, a deity, may thus be evoked equally by a *mantra*, a *yantra*, a *rāga*, or an image.

186

The complementary forms of spoken language and musical language are tied to distinct aspects of our perceptions. Musical sound, *svara*, acts on our emotional centres, whereas articulated forms, or *mantras*, belong to language and pass through our intellectual circuit. These two aspects of our perceptions relate to the two sides of our brain, connected to the channels of the subtle body known as *iḍā* and *piṅgalā*, through which our vital energies flow, joining the *mūlādhāra* to the lotus of the thousand petals at the summit of the cranium. *Iḍā*, the left-hand circuit, is called lunar. It corresponds to those aspects of our character that are considered feminine, i.e. intuitive perceptions, of which musical language is the expression. *Piṅgalā*, on the other hand, the right-hand circuit, is solar. It is considered to be active, masculine, intellectual. It concerns the *mantras*. These characteristics may be inverted according to the aspect or level of manifestation envisaged. In such cases, it is the female principle that is considered to be active, and the male principle passive. It is through the feminine aspect, through energy, the *śakti*, that the apparent world is manifested. Thus, it is through whatever is closest to the pure vibratory state, through music, that we shall be able to foreshadow something of the divine state, the state of beatitude that we cannot conceive. At the same time, the *mantra* only allows us to evoke the ideator or male principle.

Spoken language and musical language are two parallel and complementary aspects of sound language. These two forms of expression are, in fact, closely linked and inseparable. The attenuated sounds of spoken language that we call vowels are a kind of chord, or harmonic combination. Furthermore, all language uses pitch as a means of expression. If I wish to depart, for example, I may say interrogatively "Shall we go?", with a high pitch on the last syllable, and reply in the affirmative with a low pitch "Let's go". In chant or psalmody, words are mixed with the musical element properly so called. The spoken language uses pitch, accents, and elements of rhythm or duration, that belong to the musical domain. In the *japa*, the repetition of a *mantra*, *mantra-yoga* utilises certain rhythmic elements and certain characteristic numbers, whose definitions are related to those of mu-

187

sical rhythms, the *tālas*. The *gaṇas*, groupings of long or short syllables that are used as the basis for poetic metre, are identical to those
used to define the *tālas*, or musical rhythms.

Certain elements belonging to gesture — the *mudrās* — may
also contribute to articulated language. Complete language joins gesture to word and music. *Mantra* (articulated sound), *mudrā* (gesture)
and *svara* (musical sound) correspond to each other and are complementary. Rites, magical acts or *tantras*, make use of these three forms
of language, to which they add some elements of the language of
smell, such as incense, and that of taste, through the consumption of
the offerings.

It is through musical experience that each of us manages to discover the base vibration, or *Sā*, the tonic that corresponds to our
inner nature. Discovering our own *Sā*, which is the expression of our
true nature, of the position we occupy in a world where all is vibration, is an essential element in self-knowledge, the point of departure
for all knowledge. This discovery, this becoming aware of one's own
Sā, is the first exercise in a musician's training. Such an exercise may
last many months and may be extended, in practicing *yoga*, to the
search for *nāda*, the primordial sound that is the first manifestation
of the creative principle, or *Nāda-brahman* from whom the world
came forth.

In the age of the *Kali-Yuga*, in which we are now living, the way
of music, the way of the *rāga*, being a passive, intuitive way, is considered easier than that of *mantra-yoga*, which implies an active, intellectual attitude. This is one of the features of the *Kali-Yuga*, in
which the feminine aspect is favoured over the masculine in all matters concerning self-realisation and access to spiritual values.

If we examine the organs we use for sound manifestation in spoken language, we may remark that, like all the organs of our body, the
organ of speech has its symbolic characteristics. It is not by chance
that our hand has five fingers, each of which has three phalanges, that
our body has certain proportions, that our eye is solar and our ear
labyrinthine. Our organ of speech has the shape of a kind of *yantra*.
The palatine vault is like a half-sphere, similar to that of the celestial

sphere, in which we find five particular points of articulation that allow us to pronounce five main vowels, two secondary vowels and two resultant vowels, symbolically assimilated to the nine planets, two of which are as a rule invisible.

The fifty-four sounds that form the material of spoken language are classified by a mysterious formula known as the *Maheśvara Sūtra,* reflecting through the hierarchy of articulated sounds the order in which the Divine Word uttered the Universe. Nandikeśvara's commentary on the *Maheśvara Sūtra,* which is earlier than Pāṇini's Grammar in the 5th century BCE, explains this particular classification of sounds and their fundamental meaning from the most abstract point of view. We shall find its applications however in all aspects of creation, and consequently at the basis of all sciences. Nandikeśvara also indicates the correspondence between the vowels of language and musical sounds.

The nine vowels, seven main and two secondary, are paralleled by the notes of the scale, as well as the planets, colours, etc. The parallels between notes of the scale and the vowel sounds of articulated speech are evident, and both bear the same name, *svara.*

In his *Rudra Ḍamarū,* Nandikeśvara shows the correspondence between vowels and musical notes in a somewhat unexpected fashion, since he bases it on the tetrachord and not on the octave.

The *Sā,* the tonic that we shall call C for convenience, while remembering that it has no fixed pitch, corresponds to the Sanskrit vowel *a* (अ), the basis of all the others. Indeed, the tonic is the base on which all the other notes depend, and only exist because of it.

The note D, called *ṛsabha,* the bull, corresponds to *i* (इ), to energy, the *śakti.*

Next comes *Ga,* E flat, corresponding to the vowel *u* (उ), the materialised principle, the source of life, feeling and emotion.

Encompassing these three basic notes next comes E natural, corresponding to the vowel *ṛ* (ऋ)(pronounced formerly as *e* in the French "je"), meaning god personified and, in the other tetrachord, the B natural corresponding to *ḷ* (ॡ)(pronounced formerly as *u* in the French "tu"), representing *māyā,* the illusion of matter.

189

The note F corresponds to the vowel *e* (ए), the principle present in its power, its *śakti*, represented by the moon, the female symbol.

The note G is the vowel *o* (ओ), the principle present in its creation, whose symbol is the sun, the male character. The syllable AUM thus corresponds to the note G.

Then comes the note A corresponding to the open vowel *ai* (ऐ), representing the reflection of the world on its principle, hence the way of reintegration, *yoga*.

The open *au* (औ)corresponds to B flat. It evokes the universal law that determines the world's development, like a foetus in the divine womb, meaning *dharma*.

The essential basis of musical expression is thus concentrated in the first trichord: C, D, E flat. The C is the neutral basis starting from which the different intervals are constructed. The D (9/8), arising from the number 3, represents the *śakti*, and expresses movement, strength, aggressiveness. It is with E flat (6/5), arising from the number 5, that the elements life, sensitivity, emotion appear.

The consonants are formed in the same five places of articulation as the vowels, by efforts that can be directed inwards or outwards, by projection or attraction, such as the outward *k* and the inward *g*, or else the outward *t* and the inward *d*. Consonants can be "dry" (*t*), or aspirated (*th*).

All language is made up of monosyllabic entities forming autonomous elements that, added to each other, fashion complex words. The meaning of a word is the sum of the meanings of the different component syllables. Primordial language, according to Sanskrit grammarians, was essentially monosyllabic. This is the language of the *mantras*.

In this language, from which spring all the forms of language, the sounds, according to their place of articulation and the kind of effort implied, make possible the representation of the basic principles. The language of the *mantras* is thus the real language, in which a sound is the precise representation of a principle.

Thus, HAM, the guttural sound coming from *a*, is the *mantra* of ether, the principle of space-time and sphere of the sense of hearing. YAM, coming from palatal *e* is the *mantra* of the gaseous state, or air, the sphere of the sense of touch. RAM, coming from cerebral *r* , is the *mantra* of the igneous state or fire, the sphere of sight. VAM, coming from labial *u* is the *mantra* of the liquid state or water, the sphere of taste.

The last semi-vowel *l*, constitutes a separate group. The *mantra* LAM symbolises the solid state, or earth, the sphere of smell, but is also perceptible to all the other senses.

In the organ of speech, the syllable AUM is formed of guttural *a*, labial *u* and the cerebral resonance *m*. This constitutes a triangle circumscribing all possibilities of articulation, i.e. all language, and thus everything that can be expressed by language. Its multiple meanings are explained in the *Tantras* and also in some of the *Upaniṣads*, the *Cāndogya* in particular.

The *Maheśvara Sūtra* thus explains the prime meaning of all the possibilities of articulation and shows how roots can be constructed on such a basis, which, with their multiple combinations, can be used to represent increasingly complex ideas.

The different ways of pronouncing the vowels, long or short, high or low, natural or nasal, make a total of 162 distinct vowel sounds for us to shape with the aid of five groups of breathed or drawn, dry or aspirated consonants, for a grand total of thirty-three consonants. This ensemble constitutes the sum of material that can be used in spoken language. Thus, utilising Nandikeśvara's method, it is often possible to explain how words are formed in any language.

In a certain way, musical language appears more abstract, more primordial than spoken language. It is formed only by frequency ratios, vibrations, which can be reduced to pure numerical ratios. It is thus a very direct image of the manifestation process of the Word, of the world's origin, energy codes, pure vibrations, of which all the elements are formed. The mathematical principles on which musical language is based allow comparisons with the geometrical symbolism of the *yantras*, whose diagrams also serve to evoke fundamental principles, deities, and are the basis of all sacred art.

The fact that we can only recognise and reproduce exactly fifty-four distinct sounds in an octave is not the result of chance, but comes

from the fact that we can only appreciate directly certain simple numerical ratios, corresponding to different combinations of the factors
2, 3 and 5. In Indian music, in principle, only twenty-two of these
sounds are used, twenty-four if the tonic and octave are counted, but
this is in relation to a single base note. As soon as the base note changes,
the other intervals appear.

The sounds of musical language are tied to affective elements
and act directly on our psychism, creating various emotional states
called *rasas*, such as love, tenderness, sadness, fear, heroism, horror, or
peace.

Our different forms of perception also correspond to the structures of matter and life, the one only existing in relation to the other.
Thus there are parallels between colours and sounds, between planets
and the notes of music. These are no arbitrary attributions, but are
based on the observation of identical characteristics evoking cosmological principles linked to the very nature of the world. Whether we
represent the birth of the world as a cry, as a word in accordance with
the theory of the Word, or as an explosion of energy, or initial Big
Bang, the question is the same. The world develops within the limitations of certain possibilities, according to a plan — that we might term
a genetic code — and all its aspects with the same origin necessarily
have parallel structural elements. Indeed, it is through these parallelisms
that we can get some idea of the nature of the world. They are the
object of all research, of all true science. Perception and its object are
strictly co-ordinated, come from the same principles, are made for
each other and are closely inter-dependent. This is why we possess a
distinct sense to perceive each of the states of matter or elements.

The geometrical figures that form the *yantras* possess a system of
symbolic relations parallel to those of musical sounds and articulated
sounds, or *mantras*.

The parallels that can be established between colours and musical notes are complex, since they differ according to the *śrutis*, or
micro-intervals. They depend on relations between sounds and not
on their absolute pitch. In modal music, we have first to consider the
unvarying notes that form the framework of the *rāgas*.

If we consider C as tonic, as *Sā*, it appears multi-coloured. It corresponds to the point in *yantras*, and to nasal resonance or *anusvāra* in *mantras*.

The upward pointing triangle is the symbol of fire, considered in this case as the male principle. Its colour is red and it corresponds to D on the scale, to the vowel *i* of the *mantras*.

The downward pointing triangle is the symbol of water, here considered as the female principle. Its colour is mother of pearl and it corresponds to the moon, to the note F, to the vowel *ḷ* of the *mantras*.

The *Śrī Yantra*, a sacred diagram with many meanings, including that of simultaneously luminous and sonorous vibration, which is the vehicle of the universal manifestation of the Principle, whose first determination is symbolised by the central point.

The circle, a solar symbol, corresponds to the note G, to the colours black or gold, and to the *r* of the *mantras*.

The square, the symbol of earth, is yellow. It evokes the sense of smell and corresponds to the note A.

All the other notes of the scale are mobile. According to their *śruti*, their exact relation to the tonic corresponds to a colour which is that of the *śruti* category, the *śruti-jāti*, to which they belong, determining their expressive value, or feeling, the *rasa* that they evoke.

The *śrutis* are divided into five categories, corresponding to the different *rasas*, or kinds of emotion they cause. They may thus evoke a feeling of calm joy (blue), or aggressiveness (red), eroticism (orange), vanity (green), trust (yellow), melancholy (grey), fear or repulsion (violet). Thus the E, the harmonic third, is blue, while E sharp, obtained by fifths, is orange.

The overlapping triangles, that we call Solomon's seal, represent the union of opposites, the union of the sexes, as does also the cross, whose vertical line is the symbol of fire, the male principle, and whose

193

horizontal line represents water, the female principle. In music, this symbol corresponds to the ratio of G (ratio 3/2) and of F, the female symbol (ratio 2/3).

The star-shaped pentagon is the symbol of life, the sign of Śiva. In music it corresponds to E flat and to the series of expressive intervals in which the factor 5 is represented, of which the minor harmonic third is the most representative.

It is these slight differences in sounds that give music its profound psychological action. Following the *śrutis* selected for a given scale, any melodic form constructed on this scale will have a calming, pacifying effect, or on the contrary, stimulating. It is not a matter of chance that martial music utilises instruments such as trumpets, which can only give sounds belonging to the red series, aggressive and stimulating.

To obtain a strong and lasting psychological action, the modal system, as in Indian or Iranian music, is by far the most effective. The reason for it is simple: since the base note, or tonic, is fixed during the musical performance, each interval — let us say a third or a fifth — will always provide the same sound, at the same frequency. This sound is consequently repeated, returns, always charged with the same meaning. Gradually, such repeated action has an in-depth effect. If, by way of example, we are dealing with a calming blue third, the audience will gradually feel relaxed. If, on the contrary, an aggressive third is used, it will stimulate them, shake them out of their apathy, they will feel more energetic, more enterprising. Sound categories act somewhat like drugs. This is why only the modal system provides real therapeutic action and can be used efficaciously in music therapy — clearly so long as sounds themselves are very precise. We are sometimes startled by the maleficent sounds too often used in contemporary music.

The question that arises is whether such rapprochements revealing essential aspects of the nature of creation are arbitrary or coincidental, or whether, on the contrary, they are constant. In any case, they relate to the limitations that determine our perception of the world. Such questions, which may appear difficult to solve, pose no problem for Hindu theoreticians, who explain that these correspond-ences reveal the power of the *mantras*, as well as the psychological action of musical intervals.

It is easy to consider, as has often been the case, these theories and their related correspondences as being arbitrary. It must also be said that these principles, having been misunderstood, have frequently been applied in a too whimsical, if not absurd, manner. We must recall the classification made by a Chinese philosopher who, know-ing that there are five elements, defined them as earth, water, fire, silk and bamboo. Through the experience of *yoga*, we can verify the real-ity of certain fundamental factors, and in musical practice, we can experiment with the psychological action of sounds and the link be-tween our perceptions and numerical factors, independently of any theoretical approach.

Indian cosmology is a method which, instead of starting from the experience of the senses in an attempt to go back to first princi-ples, begins, on the contrary, by seeking the universal principles that find application in the various aspects of the visible and invisible world. This approach is known as *sāṁkhya*, the "study of the measur-able", a definition that indeed corresponds to the one given nowa-days to science by scholars and philosophers. Applied to articulated or musical language, it can be used to establish the relations between sounds, ideas and emotional states, something that no other method has been able to explain. Studying the parallels between the various aspects of the apparent world prepares the way for communication, through the magical power of sound, gesture and symbol, with the various states of being, with mankind, as well as between mankind, the spirits and the gods. We can go beyond the barriers of the senses and reach, at the bottom of our own selves, that transcendent reality that is the essential and ultimate goal of *yoga*.

CORRESPONDENCES OF THE NOTES OF THE SCALE

Correspondences vary according to different authors. Here we
follow the suggestions of Nandikeśvara in his treatise on language.

· u is pronounced like "u" in "put"
· ḷ like u in the French "tu"
· ṛ like e in the French "je"

Sā-Ṣaḍja (Forefather of the Six)						
⊙ C	1/2	a	ether	HAṂ HĪṂ	multi- colour	peacock
Puruṣa (Ideator Principle)						

Ṛṣabha (Bull)						
△ ☆ D	9/8 (3²/2³)	i	fire	RAṂ KLĪṂ (*kāma-bīja*)	red	ram
Kāma-bīja (Seed of desire, creative impulse) *Śiva*, male principle						

Ga-Gandhāra (Scented)						
▽∿∿ Eb	6/5 <u>(2x3)</u> 5	u	water	VAṂ ŚRĪṂ	white	crocodile
Viṣṇu, Incarnate principle, emotion, feeling *Śakti*, Female principle						

196

Ma-Madhyama (Centre or Measured)						
◡ F	4/3 (2^2/3)	e	moon	ATHA AIM	yoni nacreous	frog
Principle present in its creation, sperm						

Pa-Pañcama (Resplendent or Fifth)						
◯ G	3/2	o	sun	AUM	linga orange	heron
Cit-kāla, Conscious, acting principle *Iśvara*, Sovereign god personified						

Dha-Dhaivata (Subtle, Perfidious)						
☐ A or A+	5/3 27/16 (3^3/2^3)	ai	earth	HAIM GAM	yellow	elephant
Gaṇeśa, Reflection of the world on its creator, *yoga*						

Ni-Niṣāda (Accomplishment, Finality)						
⬡ Bb	9/5 (3^2/5)	au	air	HAUM YAM	black	antelope
Sarasvatī, knowledge, *dharma* (Universal Law)						

197

Antar-Ga (Interior or Alternative)						
☆ E	5/4	ṛ		PREM	blue	Chataka bird
(power of enchantment) Presence of the subtle in matter, *tantra*, magic						

Kakāli-Ni (Gentle, Secret)					
⬠ B	$\dfrac{15/8 \ (5\times3)}{2^3}$	ḷ		LAṂ HRĪṂ (*Māyā bīja*)	cuckoo, nightingale
Māyā, illusion, beauty, *kalā* (art)					

~24~

Publication of Sanskrit Treatises on Music and Research on Musical Phenomenology

For over twenty years, I have been working with the aim of discovering and publishing the vast Sanskrit literature on musical theory. This literature is of considerable interest because India is the only ancient country whose musical culture has continued without interruption for more than two thousand years. It is consequently in this Indian tradition that we can find the information which will one day give us a better understanding of the music of Greece, and ancient Iran, as well as the sources of Middle Eastern music and the mediaeval music of the West.

Sanskrit literature on music largely comprises manuscripts scattered throughout the public and private libraries of India, most of which have never been properly catalogued. As often as not, the identification and titles of these works are erroneous. I have thus had to explore patiently through many libraries to identify the works. It was then necessary to microfilm the most important ones, and make transcriptions of them in classical Sanskrit writing (since many of the texts were in archaic writing or in local alphabets).

These transcriptions have been classified and analysed. Many of the texts were single manuscript copies (such as the *Gītālaṁkāra*, which I have just edited) and full of copy errors, and could only be edited with the aid of borrowings from and parallels encountered in other texts of different eras. All the texts, which are always in verse, have had to be indexed, verse by verse, in order to find parallels. Furthermore, since their technical terminology cannot be found in dictionaries, an index of all the terms and their definitions at the various periods has had to be compiled, forming a dictionary of technical terms on music, which I hope one day to publish.

Currently, my material includes about 1,000 texts and 300,000 index cards.

For this work I have needed many assistants and considerable material, on which I have employed all the financial means I had. My salary as an Indian university professor and some Swiss funding allowed me to devote about two and a half million French Francs every year, making a total of around 50 million old Francs [aprox. 72,500 •].

When political conditions in India reached their current development, I deemed it prudent to give up my university post in Banaras and at the research department, which I was directing. I attempted to recreate a team at the Adyar Research Institute in Madras, to whose directorship I was appointed. The enormous work I had to do as librarian and editor of Sanskrit works, as well as a bulletin of oriental studies, unfortunately prevented me from continuing my research. I then accepted a post at the *Institut d'Indologie* in Pondichery, but failed to find the work facilities I had been counting on.

Just as I was starting on the final editing work (two particularly difficult ancient texts published and translated), I had to give it up. Manuscripts and index are now locked up in cupboards in Pondichery, waiting for me to find a place to take them, and the possibility of having one or two of my Indian assistants. No one can take up this work after me, because it needs many years of highly specialised training in music, musicology and Sanskrit.

The same goes for my instruments. I have had several experimental instruments made for measuring sounds, which have allowed me to do some serious work on oriental music. These instruments have been damaged while being transported and cannot be used for the time being. Unique and costly, these instruments are of considerable interest in studying the various musical systems, as well as for experiments in modern music.

I had hoped that it would have been possible for me to set up a laboratory in France so that I could continue my work. Unfortunately, I no longer have the financial means I had in India. The choice before me today is either to abandon a task to which I have devoted so many years, or to accept the offers I have received from foreign universities, where I may not be able to continue any serious work.

My research on the phenomenology and physical theory of music, as well as their application in comparative musicology, has been of considerable interest to contemporary musicians, musicologists, ethnologists and even psychologists and medical men.

André Jolivet has told me what I have heard from many other musicians, that he constantly uses my book on comparative musicology for his course. Pierre Boulez has asked me several times when he could work with my instruments. Many students of musicology and ethno-musicology have asked to work with me. I believe that there is a general interest in the working methods I have formulated, and of which I am practically the creator.

The Semantic

For centuries, the so-called tempered scale in use in western countries has drastically limited the composer's and performer's scope of expression. It should be remembered that the tempered scale is merely a compromise reached to facilitate the manufacture of certain instruments. It can be observed that when a performer is free to do so, i.e. vocally or using the violin, intervals are produced that are not found in the tempered scale.

The result of years of research and experiment in Indian modal music and other musical traditions of the Orient, Alain Daniélou's books *Sémantique Musicale* and *Music and the Power of Sound** advance a revolutionary theory concerning pitch ratios. Without going into details, the main concepts are as follows:

According to the author, the brain immediately classifies the factors 2, 3 and 5 and some — even quite high — multiples or products of the same, but ceases to function when fed with prime numbers higher than 5. Thus, the human ear identifies and classifies pitch according to base 2, base 3 and base 5 systems. Alain Daniélou consequently recommends dividing the octave into 52 intervals, the ratio of each note (i.e. the ratio of its pitch to the pitch of the keynote) being related to a combination, in fractional form, of the numbers 2, 3 and 5.

Each interval in Alain Daniélou's scale corresponds to a different feeling and the scale itself can be qualified as "natural", since it is

---

* An Indian edition of this book exists under the title *Introduction to the Study of Musical Scales*. See Bibliography.

202

based on simple integer ratios of frequencies found in the prime harmonics of most sounds. In other words, such intervals give rise to definite and apparently universal emotional reactions. Furthermore, according to Alain Daniélou, the Hindu theory concerning *śrutis*, or intervals, and classes of *śruti* — known as *jātis*, attributes to each interval a well-defined expressive content and classifies the intervals in easily understandable categories, which can only be explained by the nature of the numerical ratios of the cycles 2-3-5.

Moreover, the simpler the fractional ratios (i.e. the fewer multiples and products of 2, 3 and 5 they include), the greater the emotional content of the related intervals

The Semantic

Developed on the initiative of Alain Daniélou and at his request, and tuned according to his theory, the Semantic is an electronic musical instrument designed by Michel Geiss, Christian Braut, and Philippe Monsire. It is the successor of a previous version, the S 52, created by Claude Cellier and André Kudelski. The S 52 was devised to check the theory, but as an instrument was difficult to play, due to ergonomics.

The Semantic has been designed as a complete musical instrument. To make it easier to play, Alain Daniélou decided to utilise only 36 of the 52 notes of the scale (cf. Annex 2), considering the other notes less essential.

The Semantic is a "ready-to-play" instrument, fully self-contained, and user-friendly for composers and musicians. The instrument comprises a Kurzweil K 2000 R sound generator and two Midy 20 Cavagnolo button keyboards. It incorporates a powered amplifier to avoid any need for external amplification. The Semantic will offer a choice of twenty or so different tones (the spectrums of which are designed to highlight Alain Daniélou's theory). To enhance the performance, the keyboard is velocity-sensitive (the speed with which the keys are pressed), as well as aftertouch-sensitive (pressure variations while the keys are being pressed). Furthermore, sustain and expression pedals and faders are provided to produce an effect on volume attack and release parameters, spectrum, etc.

Among other reasons, the K 2000 R was chosen because each note can be tuned to one-hundredth accuracy. In other words, at the worst, the pitch of a note programmed on this instrument can only deviate by half a hundredth from its theoretical value — a very low margin of error allowed by Alain Daniélou. By way of example, raising notes C1 (65.406 Hz) and C6 (2093.005 Hz) by one hundredth corresponds to increasing their frequency by 0.0378 Hz and 1.209 Hz respectively.

As compared to the usual piano keyboard, the Semantic's button keyboard has two distinct advantages. Firstly, its aspect is sufficiently different from the former which, to the musician's mind, is synonymous with the tempered scale. It was thought that with a new instrument like the Semantic, it would be easier to break away from accepted ideas. Furthermore, with respect to the average finger span, a greater number of notes can be reached than on a piano keyboard, which is essential considering that it has three times more notes than the piano keyboard.

The Semantic has two keyboards with 105 keys each, corresponding to a range of almost 6 octaves. At the same time, it is possible to transpose by semitones or octaves. The space required for the 105 keys is a mere 18 by 4 inches. For comparison, one octave on the Daniélou scale takes up 5.2 inches, whereas on a piano keyboard the same number of notes would need 14.4 inches, or nearly three times as much.

The Semantic

1 — 2 — 3 — 4

Interval categories and their meaning
From Alain Daniélou's book, *Sémantique Musicale*

The following table lists some notes of the "Daniélou scale". Each note is given its ratio (both in fractional form and as related to the power of 2, 3 and 5), as well as the Alain Daniélou's description of the character of the interval separating the given note from the tonic.

1) Tonic and octaves (2/1, 4/1, etc.)
Meaning : base, strength, solidity, character

2) Intervals of the cycle of fifths (3 as the numerator)				3) Intervals of the cycle of fourths (3 as the denominator)			
Meaning : active, sunlike, virile				Meaning : passive, moonlight			
Intervals of the cycle of fifths				*Intervals of the cycle of fourths*			
D	9/8	$(3^2/2^3)$	vigorous, confident	Db	256/243	$(2^8/3^5)$	gentle, affectionate, calm
E+	81/64	$(3^4/2^6)$	awake, lively	Eb	32/27	$(2^5/3^3)$	gentle, loving
G	3/2	$(3/2)$	sunlight, joyful, strong, active	F	4/3	$(2^2/3)$	peaceful, calm, tranquil, passive
A+	27/16	$(3^3/2^4)$	restless, playful	Ab	128/81	$(2^7/3^4)$	tender, gentle
B+	243/128	$(3^5/2^7)$	virile, sensuous	Bb	16/9	$(2^4/3^2)$	beauty, gentle

205

4) Intervals based on major thirds (5 as the numerator)				5) Intervals based on minor thirds (5 as the denominator)			
Meaning : emotive				Meaning : sensual, passionate			
Intervals based on major thirds				*Intervals based on minor thirds*			
D-	10/9	$(5 \times 2/3^2)$	anxious, weak, fearful	Db+	16/15	$(2^4/5 \times 3)$	erotic, loving, amorous
E	5/4	$(5/2^2)$	loving, pleasing	Eb+	6/5	$(3 \times 2/5)$	passionate
F-	320/243	$(5 \times 26/35)$	doubt, unstable	F+	27/20	$(3^3/5 \times 2^2)$	aggressive, dangerous
F#	45/32	$(5 \times 3^2/2^5)$	uncertain, emotional	F#+	64/45	$(2^6/5 \times 3^2)$	active, vital, passionate
A	5/3	$(5/3)$	soft, calm	Ab+	8/5	$(2^3/5)$	amorous, enterprising
B	15/8	$(5 \times 3/2^3)$	soft, pleasing, loving	Bb+	9/5	$(3^2/5)$	desire, erotic, anxiety

6) Intervals based on double major thirds (5x5 as the numerator)			
Meaning : intense emotion, sadness			
Intervals based on double major thirds			
Db-	25/24	$(5^2/3 \times 2^3)$	sad, distressed
Eb-	75/64	$(5^2 \times 3/2^6)$	sad, disconsolate
F#-	25/18	$(5^2/3^2 \times 2)$	intensely painful
Ab-	25/16	$(5^2/2^4)$	deep sorrow
Bb-	225/128	$(5^2 \times 3^2/2^7)$	hopeless, resigned

Christian Braut

ALAIN DANIÉLOU
A BRIEF BIOGRAPHY

Alain Daniélou was born at Neuilly-sur-Seine (Paris) on October 4th 1907. His mother, Madeleine Clamorgan, descended from an old and noble Norman family. She was an ardent catholic and founded a French religious order, as well as the famous "Sainte Marie" teaching establishments. His father was an anti-clerical Breton politician, and was several times a Government minister. Alain Daniélou's brother took clerical orders and was made a cardinal by Pope Paul VI.

Alain Daniélou spent most of his childhood in the countryside, with tutors, a library and a piano. During these years, he discovered music and painting. He then left France to attend an American school in Annapolis, where he earned pocket-money by selling his paintings and playing the piano at silent movie theatres. On his return to France, he studied singing under the famous Charles Panzéra, as well as classical dancing with Nicholas Legat (Nijinski's master), and composition with Max d'Olonne. He gave recitals and exhibited his paintings.

A keen sportsman, Alain Daniélou was a champion in canoeing and an expert driver of fast cars. In 1932, he made a trip to explore the Afghan Pamir, and, in 1934, an endurance test by car from Paris to Calcutta. In between, he stayed with Henry de Monfreid in his fief of Obock on the Red Sea. Between 1927 and 1932, he met Jean Cocteau, Jean Marais, Serge Diaghilev, Stravinsky, Max Jacob, Henri Sauguet, Nicholas Nabokov, Maurice Sachs, etc. and took part in the artistic effervescence of the period.

Along with the Swiss photographer, Raymond Burnier, he then departed for the East, travelling in North Africa, the Middle-East,

India, Indonesia, China and Japan. He finally settled in India, initially with Rabindranath Tagore, who entrusted him with missions to his friends (Paul Valéry, Romain Rolland, André Gide, Paul Morand, Benedetto Croce) and appointed him director of his school of music at Shantiniketan.

Following that period, Alain Daniélou retired to Banaras, living in a mansion on the banks of the Ganges (Rewa Kothi). In Banaras, he discovered the traditional culture of India, into which he was gradually initiated. He was to stay there for fifteen years. He studied classical Indian music with the prestigious master Shivendranath Basu, and learned to play the *vīṇā* like a professional. He also studied Hindi, which he spoke and wrote as fluently as his own mother-tongue, Sanskrit and philosophy, with masters who were among the highest authorities of tradition. They introduced him to the famous *sannyasi*, Swami Karpatri, some of whose writings he translated. Karpatri initiated him into the rites of Shaivite Hinduism, under the name of Shiva Sharan ("protected by Śiva").

In 1949, he was appointed professor at the Banaras Hindu University and director of the College of Indian Music. He corresponded with René Guénon about the philosophic and religious approaches of Shaivite Hinduism.

Greatly interested in the symbolism of Hindu architecture and sculpture, of which he made a thorough study, he made long trips with Raymond Burnier to Khajuraho, Bhuvaneshvar, and Konarak, as well as to many lesser-known sites in Central India and Rajputana.

In 1954, he left Benares to take up the post of director of the Adyar Library of Sanskrit manuscripts and editions in Madras. In 1956, he was made a member of the Institut Français d'Indologie in Pondicherry, and subsequently of the École Française d'Extrème-Orient, of which he had been an honorary member since 1943.

Involved with those who were fighting for the departure of the British, as also with the Nehru family (in particular Mrs. Vijayalakshmi Pandit, Nehru's sister), the poetess Sarojini Naidu and her daughters, his sympathies lay with the independence movements. After the independence of India, however, when the new government attacked

208

orthodoxy, it was suggested that his role would be more useful in the West in presenting the true face of Hinduism.

He thus returned to Europe and, in 1963, with the help of the Ford Foundation, created the International Institute for Comparative Music Studies, in Berlin and Venice. By organising concerts for the great musicians of Asia and by publishing record collections of traditional music, under the aegis of Unesco, he played a major part in the West's rediscovery of Asian art music. For artists like the violinist Yehudi Menuhin, or the sitarist Ravi Shankar, his work was decisive in having India's classical music recognised, not just as folk music as it had been classified up to then, but as a great and masterly art on the same level as western music.

He has published seminal works on religion (*Hindu Polytheism / The Myths and Gods of India*), society (*Virtue, Success, Pleasure and Liberation, The Four Aims of Life*), music (*The Ragas of Northern Indian Music, Music and the Power of Sound*), sculpture and architecture (*Visages de l'Inde Médiévale, Le Temple Hindou, La Sculpture Érotique Hindoue, L'Érotisme Divinisé*), tales (*Tales from the Ganges, Tales from the Labyrinth*), a history of India, and a book on Yoga. His dual but by no means syncretic culture gave Alain Daniélou an outsider's view of the Western world, which can sometimes surprise. In two of his works, *Gods of Love and Ecstasy, The Tradition of Shiva and Dionysus* and *While the Gods Play - Shaiva Oracles and Predictions on the Cycle of History and the Destiny of Mankind*, he deals with the problems of a Western culture that has gone astray, having lost its own traditions and estranged man from both nature and the divine. He demonstrates that the ancient rites and beliefs of the Western world are very close to Shivaism and can be clearly explained with the aid of texts and rites existing in India.

Many of his works have been published recently, in particular the translation of the Tamil novel *Manimekhalai, The Dancer with the Magic Bowl*, a set of Italian short stories, *Tales from the Labyrinth*, a work on the *Phallus Cult* and his complete translation of the *Kama Sutra*, which was published in 1994 with great success. Most of his books are published concurrently in the U.S., including his memoirs, *The Way to the Labyrinth* : *Memoirs from East and West*. Also ready for publication are eighteen *Songs by Rabindranath Tagore* (original Bengali texts and melodies), with transcription, translation and piano arrangement by Alain Daniélou.

In 1987, on the occasion of his "four-score years", Paris fêted him, organising a show in his honour at Espace Pierre-Cardin on the Champs Elysées, in the presence of the Director General of Unesco and numerous friends from the world of art and culture.

Alain Daniélou largely divided his time between Rome, Lausanne, Berlin and Paris, his preference being for a large house hidden among the vineyards of the hills of Lazio, close to Rome.

In his latter years, he resumed his painting activities, and his water-colours have been regularly exhibited in Paris.

Alain Daniélou collaborated as musical consultant on several films, including one by Roberto Rossellini (a documentary on India), and by Jean Renoir (his great classic " *The River*"). Extracts from his recordings have been used by many film directors, choreographers (Béjart for *Bhakti* and other works), and on television and radio in many countries.

Three video programmes have been produced: *La Voce degli Dei* by the Televisione della Svizzera Italiana (Lugano, 1995), *Shiva Sharan* by A.M.Masquin (Paris 1987) and the literary programme *Apostrophe* (INA, Paris 1981).

Alain Daniélou was an Officer of the Légion d'Honneur, Officer of the Ordre National du Mérite, and Commander of Arts and Letters. In 1981, he received the Unesco/CIM prize for music, in 1987 the "Kathmandu" medal from Unesco. He was an honorary member of the International Music Council, honorary chairman of the Institutes of Music in Berlin and Venice, and was elected "Personality of the Year" in 1989. In 1991 he was awarded the Cervo Prize for new music and in 1992 he was appointed member of the Indian National Academy of Music, Dance and Theatre, being also appointed in the same year Emeritus Professor by the Senate of Berlin.

210

His books have been published in twelve countries, in English, French, German, Italian, Spanish, Portuguese, Dutch and Japanese.

He died in Switzerland on 27 January 1994 and, like the true Hindu that he was, left instructions that his remains should be cremated.

Alain Daniélou was a solitary thinker, who cannot be linked to any Western school, whether political, philosophical, or religious. He vehemently opposed the most commonplace ideologies and was a severe judge of the West. He fought for racial and cultural respect and for a harmonious and coherent caste society, largely rejecting the concepts of a levelling and egalitarian democracy. His banner was freedom, difference and pluralism, all of which are against the tide of fashion and current slogans, with the result that much of his work, lacking the support of any important lobby, remains recondite. It offers, nevertheless, original ideas and solutions to problems that the West seems unable to provide.

Overwhelmingly convinced of the importance of culture and religion as presented by Hinduism, Alain Daniélou always considered himself a Hindu and, in his last interview, declared "India is my true home".

In the recent supplement to his memoirs, he wrote "The only value I never question is that of the teachings I received from Shaivite Hinduism, which rejects any kind of dogmatism, since I have found no other form of thought which goes so far, so clearly, with such depth and intelligence, in comprehending the divine and the structures of the world."

Jacques Cloarec

Alain Daniélou's Musical & English Bibliography

Latest update on the site www. alaindanielou.org

A- Music:

Catalogue of Recorded Classical and Traditional Indian Music

Unesco, 1952.

Three Songs of Rabindranath Tagore

Original Bengali Texts and Melodies, transcription, translation and piano accompaniment by Alain Daniélou, Ricordi France, 1961.

The Situation of Music and Musicians in the Countries of the Orient

In collaboration with Jacques Brunet, translated by John Evarts, L.S. Olschki Editore, Firenze, 1971.

Introduction to the Study of Musical Scales

Published by The India Society, London
Printed by A. Bose, Indian Press LTD, Banaras, 1943.
New print by Munshiram Manoharlal Publishers, 1979.

Northern Indian Music

Barrie and Rockliff, London, 1951, 1955, 1968.
Two volumes with sanskrits texts.

Reprinted under the title *The Ragas of Northern Indian Music* - One volume without sanskrit texts, in collaboration with the International Institute for Comparative Music Studies, Berlin. Reprint : Munshiram Manoharlal, New Dehli, 1980.

"Has much to offer anyone interested in the various aspects of the music of India."
    J. Murray Barbour, Journal of the Music Division of the Library of Congress

Music and the Power of Sound
The Influence of Tuning and Interval on Consciousness

Inner Traditions International, Rochester, USA, 1995.
U.S. edition of *Introduction of the Study of Musical Scales*, with new introduction by Sylvano Bussotti.

"Much research has gone into the writing of this illuminating and fascinating book and the author knows the technique of packing a wonderful amount of information in a short compass."
    Amrita Bazar Patrika, March 1944.

"It opens a major matter and offers believable information about it."
    The New York Review of Books

Eighteen Songs of Rabindranath Tagore

Bengali Texts and Melodies by Rabindranath Tagore, transcription, translation and realisation for voice and piano by Alain Daniélou, Editions Michel de Maule, Paris, 2002.

Sacred Music. Its Origins, Powers, and Future.
Traditional Music in Today's World

Articles and speeches selected and presented by Jean-Louis Gabin, English translation by Kenneth Hurry, Indica Books, Varanasi, India, 224 pages, 2002.

In French (Music):

La Musique du Laos et du Cambodge

Institut Français d'Indologie, Pondichéry, 1957.
Out of print.

Tableau comparatif des intervalles musicaux

Institut Français d'Indologie, Pondichéry, 1958.
Distribution: Motilal Banarsidass, New Delhi.

Dhrupad

Poèmes classiques et thèmes d'improvisation des principaux râga de la musique de l'Inde du nord, notés et traduits du Vrajä Bhâshâ, du Panjabi, du Hindi et du Pûrvi, avec un avant-propos.
Les Cahiers des Brisants Éditeur, Mont-de-Marsan, 1986.

Textes des Purâna sur la théorie musicale

Institut Français d'Indologie, Pondichéry, 1959, 1987.
Distribution: Motilal Banarsidass, New Delhi.

Le Gîtâlamkâra

L'ouvrage original de Bharata sur la Musique, Institut Français d'Indologie, Pondichéry, 1959, 1987.
Distribution: Motilal Banarsidass, New Delhi.

Sémantique musicale, essai de psychophysiologie auditive

Préface de Fritz Winckel, Hermann, Paris, 1978.

Inde du Nord, les traditions musicales

avec illustrations, Buchet-Chastel, Paris, 1985; nouvelle édition : *La Musique de l'Inde du Nord*, Fata Morgana, Saint-Clément, 1995.

Origine et pouvoirs de la musique

Recueil d'inédits, d'articles et conférences. Collection "Les Cahiers du Mleccha", Kailash Éditions, Paris-Pondichéry, 2002.

B- ABOUT INDIA :

The Congress of the World

With miniatures of tantric cosmology, introduced by Alain Daniélou, translated by John Shepley, illustrated, Franco Maria Ricci Editore, Parma, 1981.

Shiva and Dionysus
The Omnipresent Gods of Transcendence and Ecstasy

Translation by Kenneth F. Hurry, Inner Tradition International, New York, 1984.

Hindu Polytheism

With sanskrit texts and illustrations, Bollingen Fondation, Princeton University Press, Princeton 1964, Inner Tradition International, New York, 1985.
New edition without sanskrit texts under the title: **The Myths and Gods of India**.

While the Gods Play
Shaiva Oracles and Predictions on the Cycle of History and the Destiny of Mankind

Translation by Barbara Bailey, Michael Baker and Deborah Lawlor, Inner Traditions International, New York/Rochester, 1987.

Fools of God

Translation of one of the **Tales from the Ganges**, Hanuman Books, Madras and New York, 1988.

Manimekhalai, the Dancer with the Magic Bowl

By Merchant-Prince Shattan, Translated from the Tamil by Alain Daniélou, with the collaboration of T.V. Gopala Iyer, co-translator : Kenneth F. Hurry, New Directions New York, 1989.

Manimekhalai's interests are wide-ranging. They lie primarily in the ex-position of Buddhism that is offered by the preacher Aravana Adigal and of the many other contemporary schools of thought co-existing in ancient India.

Rajeswari Sunderrajan. India Review of Books, Oct 29, 1994.

Yoga, Mastering the Secrets of Matter and the Universe

Unexpurgated version with sanskrit texts and new introduction, Inner Traditions International, Rochester, USA, 1991.

Original Sanskrit texts, a bibliography, and illustrations are included in the book, which is the most scholarly, detailed, and concise account of the aims, methods, results, and various forms of Yoga yet published in this country.

Mark Holloway, *Enquiry.*

The Myths and Gods of India. Hindu Polytheism

Illustrated Edition, Inner Tradition International, New York, 1991.

Not only this work has remarkable value as a mine of information; it emphasizes that aspect of the Indian in which religion and philosophy are indissolubly linked.... It is Hinduism in its entirety, seen from a particular point of view, which it presents to us.

Professor Louis Renou, *Diogenes.*

Gods of Love and Ecstasy
The Tradition of Shiva and Dionysus, The Omnipresent Gods of Transcendence and Ectasy

Inner Tradition International, New York, 1992.
New edition of: *Shiva and Dionysus.*

Virtue, Success, Pleasure and Liberation

Traditional India's Social Structures
The Four Aims of Life in the Tradition of Ancient India
Inner Traditions International, Rochester, USA, 1993.

Shilappadikâram, The Ankle Bracelet

By Prince Ilangô Adigal, classical Tamil literature, translation from the Tamil with the collaboration of R.S. Desikan, New Directions, New York 1965, Penguin Classics, India, 1993.

The Complete Kama Sutra

Treatise of Eroticism by Vâtsyâyana, with the **Jayamangalâ**. Commentary in Sanskrit by Yashodhara and Excerpts from a Commentary in Hindi by Devadatta Shastri.
The first unabridged modern translation of the classic Indian text. Translated from Sanskrit and Hindi by Alain Daniélou, translated into English by Kenneth F. Hurry. Inner Traditions International, Rochester, USA, 1994.

The Hindu Temple : Deification of Eroticism

This text translates and amalgamates two of his texts: *L'Érotisme divinisé* and *Le Temple hindou*, translated by Kenneth F. Hurry, Inner Traditions International, Rochester, USA, 2001.

A Brief History of India

The first English translation of the second edition of the work awarded the French Academy Prize in 1972, translation by Kenneth Hurry, Inner Traditions International, Rochester, USA, 2003.

The Livestock of the Gods. Tales from the Ganges

Available translation, ready for print.

Indian Metaphysics
Basic Writings of Swami Karpatri

The Mystery of the great Goddess. The Ego and the Soul. The significance of Linga-Worship. Introduction by Alain Daniélou
Ready for print.

Living in India

Available translation, ready for print, Illustrated with 64 photographies of Indian life with short notes in English, French and Italian.

Tales from the Labyrinth

Available translation, ready for print.

C- OTHERS:

The Way to the Labyrinth - Memories from East and West

Presentation by Jacques Barzun, translated by Marie-Claire Cournand, New Directions New York, 1987.

This book sings of the joy of abundance when a man fulfills himself— spirit, heart, and body— without denying anything in his given nature, without remorse, without fear, and this testimony is a hymn to life.
   Le Monde, 1987

The Phallus, Sacred Symbol of Male Creative Power

Translated by Jon Graham, Inner Traditions International, 1996.

CD Rom: *Alain Daniélou, The labyrinth of a life*
Realization, June 2002

To order : see the web site www.alaindanielou.org

DISCOGRAPHY

The records listed below refer solely to the music of India and were either produced by Alain Daniélou or were published under his direction. Most of the commentaries are bilingual in French and English.

COLLECTION UNIVERSELLE DE MUSIQUE POPULAIRE ENREGISTRÉE
Edited by Constantin Brailoiu, Record II, Asia
Musiciens et Danseurs de la caste des Ahirs
Recordings Alain Daniélou, 1951, Re-edition 1984
Archives Internationales de Musique Populaire, Musée d'Ethnographie de Genève, VDE 30-426

ETHNIC FOLKWAYS LIBRARY
Religious Music of India
Recorded by Alain Daniélou for the National Council on Religion and Higher Education, 1952. P 431

MUSICAL SOURCES (Philips, Holland)
North India, Vocal Music, Dhrupad and Khyal. 6586 003

North India, Instrumental Music, Sitar, Flute, Sarangi. 6586 009
Auvidis D 8017

North India Instrumental Music, Vina, Vichitra Vina, Sarode, Shahnai. 6586 020

Suryanarayana playing the South Indian Vina. 6586 023

ANTHOLOGY OF INDIAN CLASSICAL MUSIC (1955)
Recorded by Alain Daniélou for the International Music Council
(Unesco). Introduction by Serge Moreux
Ducretet-Thomson, 1962, 320 C 096-7-8

Vol I : *Northern Indian Instrumental Music* G 1508
Vol II : *Hindusthan and Carnatic Vocal Music* G 1509
Vol III : *Instrumental and Dance Music from South India* G 1510
Editions GREM, Paris
* *TRIBUTE TO ALAIN DANIÉLOU*, new edition as a set of three compact
discs by Auvidis/Unesco, 1997. This collection received the "Diapason d'Or" award and, in March 1998, the "Grand Prix du Disque".

From this anthology :
Inde du Sud. Les Grands Classiques
Pathé-Marconi, 1976, C 066-14324, Re-edition, 1985

UNESCO COLLECTIONS

Directed by Alain Daniélou, all of which have been or will be republished as compact disks by Auvidis Paris :

MUSICAL ANTHOLOGY OF THE ORIENT (Bärenreiter-Musicaphon, Kassel).
Commentaries in English, French and German
India I : *Vedic Chanting.* BM 30 L 2006
India II : *Dance Music from South India.* BM 30 L 2007
India III : *Dhrupad by the Dagar brothers.* BM 3O L 2018
India IV : *Carnatic Music.* BM 30 L 2021

THE COLUMBIA MASTERWORKS WORLD LIBRARY
OF FOLK AND PRIMITIVE MUSIC
India 1954, SL-215

MUSICAL ATLAS (Odeon-EMI-Italiana) Commentaries in English,
French and Italian
Bengal C O64-17840
North Indian Folk Music C 064-17859

ANTHOLOGY OF NORTH INDIAN CLASSICAL MUSIC
(Bärenreiter-Musicaphon, Kassel)
Commentaries in English, French and German

Vol I : *Vocal Music, Alap, Dhamar, Khyal, Thumri.* BM 30 SL 2051
Vol II : *Vocal Music (Bhajana, Tappa), String Instruments (Vina, Sarangi), Drums (Pakhavaj, Tabla)* 30 SL 2052
Vol III: *String Instruments, Sitar, Surashringar, Surbahar, Vichitra-Vina.* 30 SL 2053
Vol IV: *String Instruments (Sarode, Dilruba), Wind Instruments (Flute, Shahnai).*

ORIGIN OF THE TEXTS
FORMING THIS BOOK

1. **The Origins of Sacred Music**
   Unpublished, lecture at the Intercultural Institute for Comparative Music Studies of Venice, 26 September 1970.

2. **Symbolism in the Musical Theories of the Orient**
   World of Music, 26 August 1977.

3. **The Magic of Sound**
   Hindustan Times, October 1950.

4. **Magic and Pop Music**
   World of Music, volume 12, number 2, 1970.

5. **Tradition and Innovation**
   Unpublished, Moscow Congress, October 1971.

6. **Modal Music and Harmonic Music**
   Unpublished, original in English, lecture at Banaras Hindu University, 1953.

7. **Can Harmony Be Introduced in Indian Music?**
   Unpublished, original in English, Silver Jubilee Conference, Stella Maris College, Madras, November 1952.

8. **Harmonic Agression**
   Unpublished, paper for the Seminar at Royan (France), 12 March 1974.

9. **The Musical Cultures of the East in the Face of Western Hegemony**
   Unpublished, lecture at the Intercultural Institute for Comparative Music Studies of Venice, 1 April 1971.

10. **Musical Nationalism and Universal Music**
    Unpublished, date unknown.

11. The Musical Languages of Black Africa
Unesco's Conference in Yaoundé (Cameroon), published in *Revue Musicale* number 288-289, Paris, 1972.

12. The Impact of Writing and Recording on Musical Creativity
Unpublished article, Hammamet Symposium, Tunisia, 21 April 1970.

13. Music in the Modern World
The Unesco "Courrier", 1965.

14. Music and Meditation
Written for a German journal of Music-theraphy, June 1973.

15. Music, an International Language?
Unpublished article, symposium at the Abbaye de Royaumont (France), 1950.

16. Popular Religious Music in the Twentieth Century
Unpublished, lecture at the Intercultural Institute for Comparative Music Studies of Venice, 11 November 1971.

17. The Training of Professional Musicians
Unpublished, Teheran Conference, Iran, 1967.

18. Improvisatixon
Unpublished article, date unknown.

19. Basic Elements in the Vocabulary of Sound
Unpublished article, date unknown.

20. Comparative Musicology : Principles, Problems, Methods
Unpublished, lecture at the Intercultural Institut for Comparative Music Studies of Venice and Berlin, 1960.

21. Categories of Intervals or *Śruti-Jātis*
The Journal of the Music Academy, Madras, vol. 17.

22. Elements of the Formation of Scales
Résonance dans les échelles musicales, CNRS, Paris, 1963.

23. Mantra. Principles of Language and Music
Cahiers de Musiques Traditionnelles, Paris, April 1991.

24. Publication of Sanskrit Treatises
Unpublished article, 1960.